I AM NOT BUT I KNOW I AM

WELCOME TO THE
STORY OF GOD

LOUIE GIGLIO

MULTNOMAH
BOOKS

I Am Not but I Know I Am
Published by Multnomah Books
12265 Oracle Boulevard, Suite 200
Colorado Springs, Colorado 80921

ISBN 978-1-60142-428-0
ISBN 978-0-307-56339-2 (electronic)

Published in the United States by WaterBrook Multnomah, an imprint of the Crown Publishing Group, a division of Random House Inc., New York.

Multnomah and its mountain colophon are registered trademarks of Random House Inc.

Library of Congress Cataloging-in-Publication Data
Giglio, Louie.
    I am not but I know I Am : welcome to the story of God / Louie Giglio. — Rev. ed.
        p. cm.
    ISBN 978-1-60142-428-0 — ISBN 978-0-307-56339-2 (electronic)
    1. Spirituality. I. Title.
    BV4501.3.G54 2012
    248—dc23

                                                            2012029296

Printed in the United States of America
2012—Revised Edition

10 9 8 7 6 5 4 3 2 1

Special Sales
Most WaterBrook Multnomah books are available at special quantity discounts when purchased in bulk by corporations, organizations, and special-interest groups. Custom imprinting or excerpting can also be done to fit special needs. For information, please e-mail SpecialMarkets@WaterBrookMultnomah.com or call 1-800-603-7051.

*To the beautiful memory and lasting legacy
of my mom, Martha Jeane Giglio.*

CONTENTS

Start

Welcome to the book with the quirky title—*I Am Not but I Know I AM*. If you're like most people, you looked at the words on the cover once or twice (or more) before (a) the meaning settled on you, or (b) out of curiosity you picked up the book to figure out what in the world this seemingly contradictory title is all about. Thankfully, you didn't (c) become so confused that you quietly put the book down (or passed it by on your e-book store) and went on your way.

I'm really glad you made it this far because I believe that soon this crazy title will be making perfect sense to you. And I hope that the truth it represents will soon be flooding your heart with a

God-sized dose of rest and meaning, redefining who you are in the very best way. I can only pray that happens in you, because it was one of the best things that ever happened to me.

As for the offbeat title, the thought of it hit me midstream a few years back as I was speaking to a conference of youth leaders from across America. I was sharing what I think is one of the most gripping scenes in Scripture, the account where God meets Moses at the burning bush. As the encounter unfolds, God calls Moses by name and, at Moses's request, reveals His name to humankind for the very first time that we know of. In this amazing divine exchange, God discloses that His name is, in fact, a little offbeat as well, announcing that His name is "I AM WHO I AM."[1]

Simply, it means God exists. God is. God has been, He is in this moment, and He always will be—God!

The point I was trying to get across in my talk is that God is everything we need.

> ## We have already achieved the greatest heights because we know I AM.

Yet, while I was speaking, I started having a minirevelation of my own. If God's name is *I AM WHO I AM,* as He confided to Moses, then my name must be *I am not.* After all, by the nature of the name and title *I AM,* the rest of us must be called something else—and that something is *I am not I AM,* or in short, *I am not.*

To say it differently, God's name is *I have always been and always will be God,* and my name is *I have never been and never will be God.* My name is *I am not.*

"Hmm. What's so good about this news?" you may be asking. After all, many of us have spent our lives trying to do more, gain more, become more influential, get ahead, and lead the way. The message of "I am not" *seemingly* comes as an affront to our pursuit of being all we can be and experiencing the very best we can achieve. Yet, the fact that our names are *I am not* does not require us to put ourselves down, but rather to embrace the fact that we have already achieved the greatest heights because we know *I AM.*

Once while I was sharing this message with a friend who was a promising professional athlete, he questioned how this "I am not" way of thinking fit with his goals in the competitive arena. He was struggling with the notion that he was supposed to embrace his smallness, when in fact his sporting role required him to be as big and strong as possible...and hopefully to be tougher, smarter, and faster than the next guy.

You may feel the same way. You have huge dreams and giant goals, and what fuels you on the journey is the belief that *you can* do more, achieve more, be more! In fact, in the cultural space you occupy you may *have* to scratch and claw to stay in the game or to be taken seriously at all.

I went on to share with my young athlete friend that coming to terms with the idea that we are each *I am not* does not mean relinquishing our dreams, setting aside our competitive desires, or settling for less than the best in every area of life. On the contrary, knowing *I AM* inspires us to excel in every area of life. Further, the power of this "I am not" message is that when we compete, and hopefully win, we can avoid the pitfall of gaining the whole world and yet losing our souls.[2]

As we will soon discover, admitting we are not God—not in control, not running anything, not responsible for everyone's well-being, not the solution for everything and everyone, not at the center of all things—doesn't belittle us; it frees us. For as small as we may be, the truth is we are known and prized by the God of all creation. He knows our name, and we know His. We have been invited into a personal relationship with the infinite *I AM WHO I AM*. What can we ever gain or accomplish that could compete with knowing the Maker and Sustainer of the world *on a first-name basis*? What on our résumés eclipses the fact that we walk with God?

And how does this "I am not but I know I AM" message change our everyday lives?

The pages that follow are an assault on two of the archenemies of the heart, two things I believe all of us wrestle with on some level: stress and meaninglessness. The first, *stress,* gets a stranglehold on us when we move through life feeling like everything (every decision, every answer, every provision, every protection) rests on our shoulders. If we, knowingly or unknowingly, view ourselves as the source of all things for all people, we slowly lose peace of mind and find ourselves staring at the ceiling late into the night trying to figure out how to hold it all together and/or medicating ourselves just to make it through the day.

Why? Because the human frame wasn't created to carry the weight of the world. That's why, in the end, stress kills. It kills laughter. Extinguishes hope. Cracks relationships. Squashes dreams. Robs health. And steals God's praise.

> ## The human frame wasn't created to carry the weight of the world.

The other enemy of the soul, *meaninglessness,* looks quite different from stress yet chokes out life with equal vigor. Meaninglessness woos us into spending our one shot at life on insignificant and trivial things. If we are not vigilant, we drift from God's glorious ambition for our lives, losing sight of anything remotely grand, trading God-instilled passion for an easier and more often traveled road. And if our hearts aren't awakened by majesty, our lives soon shrink into little bits of nothingness. Our days become filled with drama over the ridiculous; our complaints fly free at the smallest challenge or difficulty; our energy and wealth are consumed by what is fleeting; and our chatter becomes dominated by events, people, and things that won't last much longer than the morning mist.

To both stress and meaninglessness, this book says, "Enough!"

Enough of little lives led by little people, crumpling under the weight of stress. And enough of empty ambition masquerading as something grand yet marked by the numbing effects of a vacant heart. And more important, this book bids, "Welcome to the Story of God!" In other words, these pages are an invitation to something more.

I could have opted to write this book as a treatise, a legal document to be debated and defended, or an exhaustive scriptural study. Instead, I chose to tell a story, attempting to unpack this seemingly perplexing little title with narrative accounts and colorful pictures, inviting you into an already-in-motion epic account of a glorious and gracious God.

If you are willing to let go of the idea that life is all about you, you will find yourself breathing in fresh rest and living out more meaning than you've ever dreamed. And if you grasp the hand of the Almighty, and embrace the reality that His hand is holding you, I believe you will sense a tectonic shift of the soul that will reward you with a massive payoff of joy that will surprise and stabilize your heart.

And I promise the title will make more sense in the end!

Waking

Life is the tale of two stories, one tiny and frail, the other eternal and enduring. The tiny one, the story of us, is as brief as the blink of an eye. Yet somehow our infatuation with our own little story—and our determination to make it as big as we possibly can—blinds us to the massive God Story that surrounds us on every side.

It's a little like me being shocked several years ago by the reaction of two of New York City's finest as they motioned me over to their squad cars in the middle of my midmorning run. The first officer's opening line (the exact wording of which, I'm sad to say, cannot be repeated here) led to the inexcusable reply, "What does it *look* like I'm doing?"

I quickly realized I had said the wrong thing (with an ill-advised sarcastic tone), especially to a New York City cop. In a heartbeat, my hands were on the hood of his car and threats of arrest were flying all over the place. I was startled and unnerved, and though by then it was too late, my mouth was firmly shut.

"What does it *look* like I'm doing?"

To make matters worse, all I could produce in the way of identification was a hotel key card—one of those fancy ones that look cool but don't even contain the name and address of the hotel. The whole scene was going downhill fast...

Things had started off innocently enough that morning as I headed out the door of our midtown-Manhattan hotel and began plodding down the sidewalk toward the East River about eight blocks away. But just a few steps into my run, it started to rain. First it was just annoying—an intermittent, spitting kind of rain that was more of an inconvenience than anything else. But then the wind picked up, and a steady, chilling downpour started making things miserable. By now I was well on my way and too far from the hotel to make turning back a sensible option, so I kept running north along the river, pressing on in the driving rain.

I don't know what kind of shape you're in, but when I run, I usually think more about survival than scenery. And when I'm running in a cold downpour, I barely think at all. I certainly don't look around to read a lot of the signs. Thus I wasn't paying much attention when suddenly my path was blocked by a chain-link fence. The battered fence stretched from the riverbank on my right to a concrete lane divider that had been following me on my left. Once again I considered my options. Retracing my steps didn't make sense. What made sense was getting out of the rain. So without thinking I hopped over the lane divider and headed for the shelter of an overpass I now noticed across the way.

As it turns out, the overpass was elevated and continued on ahead of me. Luckily, I could keep running under cover for the foreseeable future. This was good news.

I continued north, not really noticing that the lane to my right had, at some point, become two lanes, and then three. After another mile or so, the traffic in all three lanes was moving slower than I, and a driver in one of the cars was shouting something in my direction. But in the rain and traffic, I couldn't quite make out her words. To be honest, I was trying to ignore her anyway. Then the overpass drifted away to the left, and I was once again exposed to the rain.

Soon I noticed the lower levels of the United Nations buildings on my far left, and just ahead were two police cars parked on a wide concrete median. A single officer sat in each car, their eyes meeting mine as each step I took drew us closer together.

Everything seemed to be fine, until my forward progress was interrupted by the piercing *blurp* of one of the officers' sirens and the intense motion of his hand directing me to approach.

It was at that moment that I realized I was running down the middle of the FDR, a six-lane expressway that snakes along the eastside shoreline of Manhattan. No kidding! In all my effort to keep putting one foot in front of the other, somewhat blinded by a steady rain, I hadn't noticed that my haphazard path had now placed me squarely in the middle of *a freeway*! No wonder the officer's first question when I finally splashed to a stop in front of his car was incredulous and unprintable.

I mean, seriously! How can you run down the middle of a New York City freeway and not know it? I think the same way you can live your entire life oblivious to the grand Story of the Creator of the universe, an epic tale that is unfolding all around you. The same way you can spend your days making so much of someone as small and transient as you or me and so little of someone as glorious and eternal as God.

That's why this book is not about you and making your story bigger and better, but about you waking up to the infinitely more massive God Story happening all around you…and about you discovering God's invitation to join Him in it. This book is about looking up to see that there's a Story that was going on long before you arrived on planet earth and that will go on long after you're gone.

God is the central character of this preemptive and prevailing

Story, and He is the central character of this book. Because of who He is, God commands center stage in existence, creation, time, life, history, redemption, and eternity.

It's not as though God has some kind of dictator mentality, a misguided sense of self-worth and importance that demands that everyone salute Him and call Him "Sir." Rather, God is God— the Author and Sustainer of everything. He is Alpha and Omega, the Beginning and the End. All things emanate from Him and terminate in Him. From Him alone, every living thing draws its breath. In Him alone, everything is held together.

He is great and grand beyond our ability to comprehend. And He is center stage in history, in eternity, and in all there is.

It's all about Him, and therefore, it's not about you. In saying that, I am not trying to put you down. Nor am I trying to imply that you don't matter at all. To say it's not about you isn't to suggest that you have no place in the incomparable Story of God. In fact, the opposite is true. Amazingly, you appear on every page of God's Story, existing in His thoughts long before this world was made. But we cannot lose sight of the obvious—the fact that the Story already has a star, and that star is not you or me.

Here's why that matters: if we don't get the two stories straight, everything else in our lives will be out of sync. We'll spend our days trying to hijack the Story of God, turning it into the story of us. Inverting reality, we'll live every day as though life is all about you and me. We'll live like the world is our habitation alone, existence our playground, and God our servant (that is, if we decide we need Him at all). We will throw every ounce of our energy into the fleeting story of us. Calling the shots, our me-centered thinking will dictate every move we make and how we feel.

> ## The Story already has a star, and that star is not you or me.

If we're good enough, we'll cobble together a decent little story, one in which the limelight shines on us and on all we have done. Yet in the end—when the last clap is clapped for our tiny tale—our story will fade to black, a pitiful return on our one-shot chance called "life on earth."

About thirty minutes into my ordeal with the New York police officers, the situation lightened a bit as I realized that the worst that was going to happen to me was getting a ticket for jaywalking, something I certainly deserved. As we were waiting for my vital information and my record of wrongdoing to appear on the squad car's computer, the nicer of the two cops asked me within earshot of the other, "So, what do you do for a living, anyway?"

Hmm.

Opting for the short answer, I said, "I'm a pastor."

Two sets of eyebrows rose.

"A pastor!" one of the officers blurted out while they both drew a more inquisitive bead on me. "What kind of pastor are *you*?"

I think he was looking for the name of a denomination, but I simply replied, "I'm a Christian."

"Oh yeah? Well, what are you doing in New York?"

"I'm here to speak to a group of college students tonight in Queens."

Long pause. More staring.

"So, what are you going to tell them?"

For a split second, time stood still. And then I told him, "I'm going to remind them that life is short and our time on earth is really brief. That's why we have to make sure our lives count for the stuff that lasts forever."

And that's what I want to do in these pages. My hope is to lead you to a fresh awareness of the six-lane-wide, freeway-sized God Story that you and I are running down the middle of every day.

It's an awareness that requires a constant choice. We can either choose to cling to starring roles in the little-bitty stories of us or opt to exchange our fleeting moment in the spotlight for a supporting role in the eternally beautiful epic that is the Story of God.

I want to lead you (and me) to that beautiful place of surrender, that place where we give in and give up on the story of us and step up and join in the Story of God's fame.

If such a notion unnerves you from the start, don't think of it as losing. Think of it as trading up.

Abandoning the tiny story of me and embracing the forever Story of Jesus will allow our little lives to be filled with the wonder of God as we live for the unending applause of His name. And joining our small stories to His will give us what we all want most in life, anyway: the assurance that our brief moments on earth will count for something in a Story that never ends.

Look Up

Given the unusual August heat, it's remarkably cool in here. And quiet.

At least it was until now. A noisy Italian family has just clamored past me down the aisle, oblivious to the stillness.

From where I'm sitting, it looks like Grandma, her favorite (perhaps only) son, his wife, and their three kids. They all seem instantly impressed, even the daughter, who is now fighting through her outer shell of teen-cool to pull the ear buds out of her ears. As she looks up, her mouth is wide open, her lips mouthing "W-o-w!" in slow motion for no one in particular to hear.

A rapid flurry of conversation is being exchanged among them, spearheaded by the dad, whose voice is nearing full volume. Making out the word *magnifico,* I think he just offered for the family's consideration, "Isn't this place magnificent?"

Everyone except the littlest one nods, especially Grams, who seems to be genuinely awestruck by what she sees and maybe equally moved that she is seeing it with the people she loves most. She looks to be close to seventy. A small, roundish woman with a gentle smile and sparkling eyes.

Dad, as you might expect, has the tourist look—sandals (with socks, of course), zip-off cargo pants, sunglasses perched atop a closely shaved head, and the can't-leave-home-without-it fanny pack. He's holding an open brochure that rattles in the air as he wildly gestures with his hands.

Then there's Mom—she's all classic Italian glam with her designer jeans, high heels, and superhip shades.

Isabella, the teen daughter (yes, I know her name now, as do all those within fifty feet of her dad), is trying her best to have a good time without appearing to be overly "into" the family outing. Her jeans are ragged and about four inches too long, hiding what I think are sandals underneath. A pink backpack follows her every move, as does the attached snowboard-shaped key chain that swings from side to side. Fortunately for her younger teen brother, the key chain is at just the right height for him to demonstrate his karate skills with his foot, which he does repeatedly on the way down the aisle.

And then there's little Paulie. Maybe five or six years old, he is clearly the darling of the clan. Every other second his name echoes off the walls, being constantly called by his father, mother, brother, sister, and grandma. But Paulie is zoned out in Nintendo Land, and I'm pretty sure he doesn't hear a thing. He's simply following along with a child's sixth sense, never taking his eyes off the video images dancing on the screen of the game player that's firmly in his grip.

Little does he know, he's in a place that bears his name.

Enormous and ancient, St. Paul's Cathedral is one of the world's most amazing structures, completed more than three hundred years ago in an era when the very act of coming to worship caused you to look up in awe and wonder.

Sitting here, I'm feeling pretty small.

For an hour or so, a steady stream of reverent (and some not so reverent) onlookers have come by. A multitude of faces and cultures. A tour group of about sixty. A few dozen school kids with English accents. Couples. Loners. And the fascinating little Italian family. And you know what? They've all been doing exactly the same thing—craning their necks and looking high above. And for good reason. The ceiling of this sacred hall looms *nine stories* above, giving way to one of the world's largest cathedral domes, a cavernous opening spanning more than a hundred feet—a jaw-dropping curvature of wonder rising still higher overhead.

To say this place is huge is a massive understatement. It's a football field and a half long, the dome alone weighs approximately sixty-five thousand tons, and the cross that adorns its outer shell rises 365 feet above London's Ludgate Hill, a spot of earth that has been home to a church building since AD 604.

But St. Paul's is lifting my heart and my head toward something even bigger, something higher, Someone more.

Sure, Sir Christopher Wren's architectural masterpiece is a testimony to the ingenuity, skill, and determination of human beings. But even in its grandeur, St. Paul's fails to reach near heaven, and its exterior is often shrouded by scaffolding and tarps as renovators wage a continuing battle against the corrosive powers of time. And though the cathedral miraculously survived the relentless bombings of World War II, St. Paul's will not stand forever. Yet the God this building speaks of will—a fact that seems more real than ever to me as I gaze up from my pew.

Sitting here, I'm feeling pretty small.

Granted, we shouldn't need massive buildings to evoke an awareness of grandeur in our hearts, especially given the cathedral of earth and sky we call home. Besides, the real church is those of us who believe—a Holy Spirit–infused marvel of God's constructive genius—and not the lifeless fortress of stone that encompasses me now. Just the same, this place is special, and by simply being here, I'm shrinking on the inside, listening to the constant echo that declares both bigness and smallness, His and mine.

Now a young girl is whispering excitedly to her friend, "This is where Princess Di got married!" Granted, these walls have witnessed their share of pomp and pageantry, but somehow pop culture is lost on me in this moment. St. Paul's speaks of more than history. This place is a window to eternity. It's as if the building is doing in this moment just what it was designed to do—whispering softly, "God is big. Really, really big."

And what's echoing back to me is the realization that I am not.

Sitting here, I feel so small—and small feels surprisingly good. So good that I begin to wonder why it is so surprising that feeling small can feel so good.

"God is big. Really, really big."

You would think that getting a glimpse of God's true size would have us happily lining up to embrace our humble estate, especially given the fact that we are so dearly loved by the One who gives life to us in the first place. But then again, human history is not exactly a record of humanity's unquenchable quest for smallness. More accurately, our history testifies to a continuing, insatiable quest to make our names, our fortunes, our fame, and our kingdom as vast and enduring as possible.

Unfortunately, such a quest is an exhausting proposition. For one thing, none of us seems to know when "big" is big enough, leading us up a dizzying and deceptive staircase that promises contentment while constantly beckoning us one rung higher to a state of more. But, to our unending dismay, "enough" never arrives. Even more exhausting, our preoccupation with ourselves puts us at odds with God Himself, given that any attempt to pump up our names is, in effect, an attempt to push Him from the center and steal His glory—a quest as tiring and futile as trying to extinguish the sun with an eyedropper.

The truth is, feeling small may not be so bad after all, if in recognizing our smallness, we come to realize the wonder of God—a God who is beyond our ability to fully describe or imagine, yet Someone we are privileged to know, love, and embrace. Looking up from our fragile little lives, we are faced with the supremacy of a God who is fully capable of not only running the entire cosmos today—a task that doesn't tax Him in the slightest—but of sustaining the affairs of our lives as well.

It all starts when you look up.

So, if you're at a place in life where weariness and strain are more commonplace than rest and wonder, this book has found you at just the right time. God knows you better than you know yourself. He knows just how small and frail you are. He knows you're just one person, a tiny one at that. He knows your limitations, and He made you that way for a purpose. That's why God never asks you to be more than you are—and why He always stands ready to be your constant supply.

God knows that you are weak, and He is in touch with just how potent He, Himself, is. And right now, He desires to do huge, God-sized things through you, if you're ready to abandon the quest of making more of self and to embrace the miracle of being small, yet knowing His name.

It all starts when you look up.

It's been a few minutes, but that's exactly what my Italian friends are still doing. While they're looking up, I'm wondering if they've ever seen a glimpse of heaven or if they realize they have been invited to know God intimately and join His Story.

I can't help thinking about Isabella. Obviously, I don't know her, but I gravitate toward her because she looks a lot like the students that our ministry seeks to lead. It may just be me, but I don't think there are many sixteen-year-olds who are living in a bigger story, embracing each day as if the purpose of life is a whole lot bigger than them. Sure, that's a generalization, but most teenagers are all about me and mine—my hair, my fashion, my friends, my approval and acceptance by others, my being in the right place at the right time with the right people. Funny, though young, they're not that different from the rest of us, just not yet mature enough to manage their selfishness as well as some of us older folks do. I really want Isabella to wake up to the bigger Story, because most of her life is ahead of her and she adds that sense of youthful wonder that all of us in the Story really need.

Then there's little Paulie. Oh boy. How can he *not* think life is all about him? After all, isn't that what we are saying a lot of the time to kids these days from the second they're born? But what they really need to hear at birth is, "We love you so much and want you to know we are really excited you are here. But life is not all about you! Welcome to the Story that is already in progress!"

What about Dad? I can see him on the phone, doing the deal, managing the enterprise. He thinks it's all in his hands—the business, the relationships, the equity, the direction, and the future. He loves his family, but he's married to his work. He believes in God, but in the daily flow of life, he acts like he doesn't need Him at all. He thinks he's generous, but he keeps shoving his stuff into a bigger pile. He thinks he has it all together, but the foundation is a lot shakier than he knows. At the end of the day, he's going to be dumbfounded when he finds out just how tiny he really is and discovers that God gave him life and breath and every earthly possession so that he would have something to contribute to the massive God mission that has no end.

As for Mom, I'm guessing that her story on most days is whatever is on the other end of the phone, whatever the latest raging topic is between her friends. It's like somehow she's telling me something without saying a word—"My kids have the right stuff,

I have the right stuff, we live in the right neighborhood, attend the right schools, do Mass at the right church, vacation in the right places…" I doubt she knows where she put the Story down—that is, if she ever picked it up in the first place. I wonder if she knows that God invented the stuff in Botox and that He loves her with or without it. I'm sitting here wondering if her heart is shrinking with the dying story of "her and hers," wondering if she's ever known the rush of hearing Him call her by name.

Oh yeah, I almost overlooked the middle boy. But I guess it's not the first time. He's not the prized one—like Daddy's little girl—or the precious baby boy. Everyone is always looking out for Paulie, even him. Oops. I'm not talking about the middle son, am I? He's pretty determined that sooner or later he's going to break out of the shadows and finally make something in life about him. But I hope he doesn't.

> ## I want to tell her there's a huge holy God on the other side waiting for her.

And we close with sweet little Grandma. At the family table she probably never sits down—always serving, always moving, always making sure everyone else has what they want. One minute she's making sure the lasagna is served piping hot, and the next that Paulie gets his dessert with just a little scoop of ice cream on a different plate because he doesn't like it when the dessert and the ice cream touch each other. Dad wants coffee with milk. Isabella doesn't like rhubarb, so there is a small cherry dessert for her. No wonder Grandma never sits!

My first inclination is to just give her a hug and say thank you, as she chooses most days to sacrifice self for the good of those around her. But in that moment, it hits me—sin is deceptively strong and pride has many faces.

I want to tell Grams that it's okay for her to sit and eat. I'm presuming Grandpa has already gone, and I'm guessing she wonders a lot about where he is and if she'll ever see him again. Eternity is on her mind a lot, as it should be. I want to tell her there's a huge holy God on the other side waiting for her. And encourage her that even though she will be completely floored by His glory when she sees Him, she doesn't have to be afraid. I want to tell her about the love of God and the gift of His Son.

You think Grandma's too old for all this tiny story / huge story stuff to matter? I don't. I'd remind her that Moses was older than she is now when he got a surprising invitation to look up, trade up, and step into a major role in the great Story of God.

Divine Invitation

God is always looking for ordinary people to play significant roles in His unfolding Story. And, given that He is God and supremely confident in Himself, He is free to choose the least among us—the slowest, the lesser known, the last, the smallest, the poorest—to accomplish amazing, God-sized stuff. While as humans we try to partner with the brightest and most powerful, God is simply looking for people who are willing to take Him at His Word—those confident that with Him in the equation, everything is possible.

So try to put yourself in God's position for a minute. Your people are enslaved in Egypt, toiling day and night building monuments to the fame and greatness of the pharaohs. Yet you have a redemption plan, a deliverance mission, and you're looking for a spokesperson to take your agenda to the most powerful man in the most powerful empire on the planet, demanding that he let your people go free. Who are you going to choose to lead Israel out of bondage? What criteria are you going to use to narrow the field of candidates? How will you train the person you choose to lead? How will you ensure the success of the mission?

Well, you probably wouldn't choose a stuttering shepherd with wilting self-esteem—an aging man on the downslope of life, who for years had been on the run from the mighty Pharaoh after killing one of the ruler's slave-driving foot soldiers back in Egypt. But that's exactly who God chose—that's just the guy He invited to stand at the helm in this chapter of His developing Story.[1]

I'm guessing you might already know the story I referred to from the introductory portion titled "Start." When Moses looked up, a nearby bush was on fire. But what was really strange was the fact that the bush continued to burn without being consumed. Intrigued, Moses stopped to investigate, and when he moved in for a closer look, a voice thundered out of the flames, "Moses! Moses!"[2]

Moses stopped in his tracks. God had found His man.

Not that finding Moses was all that difficult for God. He didn't have to do a Google search. He knew exactly where to find him. For even though Moses was on the backside of nowhere, that nowhere he was on the backside of was a place called Mount Horeb—a place Scripture refers to as "the mountain of God."

I AM NOT BUT I KNOW I AM

Moses probably thought he was alone with the flock for another dusty day, stranded in the wilderness, just counting the days in the closing chapters of his life. Little did he know that he was tending his sheep in God's neighborhood, or that he was about to be invited to play a major role in God's deliverance plan.

"Moses! Moses!"

In what would turn out to be a prophetic reply, Moses answered, "Here I am."

That's when Moses's world turned upside down. "Do not come any closer," God exclaimed. "Take off your sandals, for the place where you are standing is holy ground."[3]

I doubt Moses needed a second admonition. Instantly he ripped the sandals from his feet and buried his face in his hands.

Now that He had Moses's undivided attention, God laid out His plan. "I have indeed seen the misery of my people in Egypt. I have heard them crying out because of their slave drivers, and I am concerned about their suffering. So I have come down to rescue them from the hand of the Egyptians and to bring them up out of that land into a good and spacious land, a land flowing with milk and honey.... The cry of the Israelites has reached me, and I have seen the way the Egyptians are oppressing them."[4]

Did you notice all the first-person pronouns God is using to state His case? "*I* have seen." "*I* have heard." "*I* am concerned." "*I* have come down." *I'm* going to do something.

God's mind was set. His plan was in motion. Failure was not an option. No insurmountable obstacle stood in His way. God had sized up Pharaoh, a man of unrivaled political and military power, and decided to use him as a pawn in His Story. The redemption mission would go on as scheduled, Pharaoh's army notwithstanding, and a couple of million people would journey through an arid wasteland to safely arrive in the land long ago promised to their forefathers. Mark it down. It was going to happen. God was confident that the Promised Land—the place He had chosen for Israel to dwell—was suitably perfect, even if it was presently inhabited by skilled warriors defending walled cities.[5] God wasn't deterred and He didn't need assistance. But He had chosen to use a man, a human mouthpiece—someone who would carry His message and lead His cause. That's when, for Moses, the conversation took an ominous turn.

> "So now, go. I am sending you to Pharaoh to bring my people the Israelites out of Egypt."

Without taking a breath, God added, "So now, go. I am sending you to Pharaoh to bring my people the Israelites out of Egypt."[6]

What? All of a sudden the great *I AM* is going to do something amazing through someone else, someone small. Somehow the "I" pronouns evaporate, and Moses is left reeling in the wake of blatantly second-person marching orders: "So now, go."

Confused and overwhelmed, Moses blurts out, "Who am I, that I should go to Pharaoh and bring the Israelites out of Egypt?"[7]

I think the thoughts that were going through Moses's mind were the same kind that often race through your mind and mine when we're called on by God to do something that seems way beyond our abilities. *God, are You serious? Is this a joke? Have You mistaken me for somebody else? Surely You don't think I can pull this off, do You? Who, me? Do what?*

But look more closely at what God actually said to Moses.

When He told him to go and bring them out, He wasn't thinking Moses was going to actually do the delivering. God wasn't counting on Moses's skill or power to break the chains of bondage that held His people captive. God was going to do all the work. He just wanted someone in human form to speak on His behalf and lead the people to His promised destination. All along, God was counting on Himself to pull the Story off—not Moses. Definitely *not* Moses.

When God said, "So now, go," He was implying, "I am going to do this with or without you, Moses, but I've been searching for just the right partner, a regular guy who will believe that I am able to do exactly what I have said I will do. You just need to merge onto the highway of My agenda—My promised-before, now-happening, already-in-motion agenda—and watch Me go. Don't deviate from what I am saying. Trust Me. Follow Me without fear of any person. This is going to be amazing. Oh, and by the way,

I could do it all by Myself, but I'm choosing to use a human vessel—a tangible, flesh-and-blood ambassador for the cause. And I am choosing you, Moses. So now, you go!"

Sadly, in the heat of the moment, those last two words were the only ones Moses heard.

"You go!"

Immediately the questions and doubts gushed out of his mouth. "A stuttering man like me? You want me to go to Pharaoh? How? He'll kill me!"[8]

Interestingly, God didn't respond with a pep talk. He didn't send Moses to the Center for Possibility Thinking in an effort to boost his confidence. Nope, notice God didn't waste any time— not one second—trying to pump Moses up for the task. He didn't inflate Moses's self-esteem by filling him with a boatload of "Come on, Moses, you can do this! I believe in you—you've just got to believe in yourself!" encouragement.

"You go!"

Instead, God answers Moses's "Who am I?" question with five life-shifting words as He simply affirms, "I will be with you."[9]

When God invites us into His Story, assigning us various roles that are seemingly too big for us to carry out, His affirmation is always the same—*I will be with you*. So it's as if He was saying to Moses, "Don't worry about who you are. Just focus on the reality of who I am and the fact that I'm going too. And if I go with you, trust Me, everything's going to work out fine."

Bottom line: God plus anyone else is an overwhelming majority, an exceedingly powerful team.

By now, things were getting dicey for Moses, but to his credit he didn't fold up and run. After all, the bush was still a raging flame and a holy hush was hanging thick in the air. Barefoot and trembling, Moses somehow mustered the courage to ask God to produce some personal identification.

Honestly, who could blame him? It's not likely that Moses was going to go charging into Egypt, instantly gaining the trust of the Israelites while striking fear into the heart of an ironfisted dictator like Pharaoh. No, before that was going to happen, Moses knew he'd need a lot more information about the One who was sending him and who would be going with him.

"How will they know we had this conversation?" Moses stuttered. "They won't believe the burning bush thing, even if I tell them, and they won't be able to sense the otherness of Your presence like I can right now. If they say, 'And just who was this God you were talking to out in the wilderness?' what will I tell them?"[10]

Can you believe it? Moses is asking the God of all creation to tell him His name.

It's important here to grasp the gravity of the situation. Of course, God already knew Moses's name (He had repeatedly called him by his first name at the outset of this exchange). But Moses didn't know God's name. In fact, no one did. Since the dawn of time, God had been referred to as Elohim, meaning "Strong One," and Adonai, meaning "Master." But those revered titles were really more descriptions than personal names. No one knew God's personal name. And, as far as we know, no one had dared to ask.

Who would?

"I AM WHO I AM. Tell them, I AM sent me to you."

I mean, it's not as though God was just a little higher and a little more holy than Moses, someone you'd stroll up to and say, "Hey, man, what's up?" No, we're talking about the Infinite One —the One whose voice alone causes worlds to be born and grown men to hide their faces—having a conversation with a little, frail, finite creature. A creature who wants to know if he can call Almighty God by name.

God was in no way obligated to answer, yet without hesitation He did answer. To this aging, semiwashed-up shepherd, God revealed His name, saying, "I AM WHO I AM. This is what you are to say to the Israelites: 'I AM has sent me to you.'"[11]

What?

I'm pretty sure Moses didn't get it right away. In fact, he was probably thinking, *That's what I'm asking You, God. You are who?*

And the reply comes back, "*I AM* [long pause], that's who."

"Your name is *I AM*?"

"That's right, Moses, my name is *I AM WHO I AM*. My name is *I AM*."

I wonder how long it took for God's name to register in Moses's brain. Maybe he was thinking, *First name: I AM. Middle name: Who. Last name: I AM. Interesting.*

But it's more than simply a clever juxtaposition of words. God has a unique and amazing name. In Hebrew, the language of the Old Testament, the word for *"I AM"* is *Hayah,* the pronunciation of which originates deep down in the throat (think of the loud karate expression). *Hayah* carries with it the idea of the very breath of God. In the original language, God's name reflects the creative, breathing-out-all-there-is nature that He alone possesses. God's name, like God Himself, is the life-giving source of everything.

In English, the name *I AM* translates into the verb *to be*. Or more simply, *be*.

Therefore, God's name is *BE*.

I AM = *I BE*. Not great grammar, I know, but powerful theology.

God knew it was imperative for Moses to know who He was—that He was *I AM*. *I AM* is the present tense, active form of the verb *to be*. As God's name, it declares that He is unchanging, constant, unending, always present, always God.

God was telling Moses,

I AM the center of everything.

I AM running the show.

I AM the same every day, forever.

I AM the Owner of everything.

I AM the Lord.

I AM the Creator and Sustainer of life.

I AM the Title Holder of the universe.

I AM the Savior.

I AM your Source.

I AM more than enough.

I AM inexhaustible and immeasurable.

I AM WHO I AM.

I AM God.

In a heartbeat, Moses knew God's name—and something more. He finally knew his. For if God's name is *I AM,* Moses's name must be *I am not.*

I am not the center of everything.

I am not in control.

I am not the Source.

I am not the solution.

I am not all-powerful.

I am not calling the shots.

I am not the Owner of anything.

I am not the Lord.

I am not.

That's my name too. And yours. Just try it under your breath: "My name is *I am not.*"

I am not running anything.

I AM NOT BUT I KNOW I AM

I am not the head of anything.

I am not in charge of anything.

I am not the Maker.

I am not the Savior.

I am not holding it all together.

I am not all-knowing.

I am not God.

Sure, people might call you Tommy or Eddie or Amanda or Juan or Michelle or Erin or Courtney. But, let's face it, when you get right down to it, all our names are *I am not.*

And God's name is still *I AM.*

While Moses was still reeling, God continued, "This is my name forever, the name by which I am to be remembered from generation to generation."[12] In other words, God wanted Moses to know that not only would He remain the same, but also His name would endure to every generation that would inhabit earth—even to our generations, mine and yours.

> ## And God's name is still *I AM.*

I love this verse because it puts us in the Story. Oh, you may have just been calling Him God all these years—and, in fact, that's who He is. But He gladly told Moses that His name is *I AM*

(BE), and that's still His name today. Right now. Wherever and whoever you are.

God is big. We are not. He is calling the shots, directing the script, and determining the plot. We are not. And what's really wild is that while He doesn't *need* any of us, He is *choosing* to include us, inviting us into the Story that never ends.

God didn't need Moses. He chose Moses. Wow! What a subtle, yet titanic, shift of thinking. God doesn't need us to accomplish His plans. God chooses us to be included in His purposes. And when we feel the weight of being included in such God-sized undertakings, He reminds us that He is with us. Of course God believes in us. But where we often get off track—and where we put ourselves under the weight and strain—is in that moment when we start assuming that God's hopeful outcome is riding squarely on our ability to pull it off.

The Almighty believes in you. He wants to constantly affirm you. But He will never deceive you by telling you that you are more than you are.

Stunningly, the Creator is always inviting the creature into His Story. But at all times He is solely counting on Himself to write each chapter and direct the outcome!

Try to fathom it—little you and little me invited into the massive and mysterious Story of the great *I AM.* Are you up for it?

Light Flies

Light flies. If you don't believe me, go outside tonight, crank up the family car, and try to race the beam streaming from the headlights to the end of the driveway. Light is fast—really fast—traveling at 186,000 miles per second. How fast is that? In the time it takes you to snap your fingers just once, a ray of light can circle the globe seven times. Like I said, light is quick.

Light has to be fast because the universe is so big. The warmth you feel on your face when you walk outside on a sunny afternoon is light that left the surface of the sun eight minutes ago. If you wanted to repeat the 93-million-mile journey and return to the sun (not a good idea given that the temperature at the sun's surface is 10,000 degrees Fahrenheit and it would vaporize you long before your arrival), the trip would take you almost five years flying nonstop, twenty-four hours a day, in our fastest jet, traveling at a constant speed of 2,298.6 miles per hour.

I don't know about you, but for me, a beam of light covering 93 million miles in eight minutes is pretty hard to comprehend. Much less the news that a team of astrophysicists have discovered what is believed to be the farthest object from earth, a galaxy that is 13 billion light-years away.

If you want to put that distance in perspective, consider that a light-year (how far light travels in 365 days) is equal to 5.88 trillion miles. If it helps, that number again is 5,880,000,000,000 miles. That's a lot of zeros, and frankly, a number too large to really mean anything of significance to most of us. We can fathom the inch, the yard, the meter, and the mile. Most of us can get our heads around the fact that it's about two thousand miles from Atlanta to L.A., a mile being four times around the track at the local high school football field, thus L.A. being eight thousand laps from Atlanta.

But how are we supposed to grasp the idea of something blazing through the universe at roughly 186,000 miles per second, morning and night, for an entire year? A light-year—who needs it? You may be thinking, *Not me.*

Then again, astronomers—who work in an environment where miles and kilometers lose meaning—love and need the light-year in their quest to map out the cosmological landscape around us.[1] Thus the folks at the California Institute of Technology are fairly certain the aforementioned most distant galaxy is 13 billion light-years away—or 13,000,000,000 times 5,880,000,000,000 miles away. That qualifies it as the oldest visible light in all creation and the farthest thing from earth our eyes have ever seen.

But let's bring things closer to home—you know, *home,* our galactic neighborhood, the Milky Way. Our cozy little corner of space, the Milky Way Galaxy, is somewhere between 100,000 and 120,000 light-years across. So to get from one end of our neighborhood to the other, all you have to do is zoom at 186,000 miles per second for 100,000–plus years. Our galaxy is home to hundreds of billions of stars, only one of which is our sun. Our solar system is located about 25,000 light-years from the center of the Milky Way. And just as the planets in our solar system orbit our sun, so our sun and all the other hundreds of billions of stars in the Milky Way orbit around its center—a galactic revolution that takes our sun 250 million earth years to complete.

By way of a quick review…

We have no idea just how big the universe is, but it's so big we have to use a ruler that's 5.88 trillion miles long to measure stuff. The ruler is called a *light-year.*

The farthest thing we have measured so far, with the help of a mighty telescope (actually two telescopes, one in Hawaii and one in space, combining together and aided by the natural magnification provided by a massive cluster of galaxies), is 13 billion light-years away.

Somewhere in the midst of the universe is a spiral galaxy called the Milky Way, which is made up of hundreds of billions of stars.

One of those stars is our sun, warming our days from 93 million miles away.

One of the planets circling our sun is planet earth.

Earth makes its journey around the sun once every year, while together the earth, sun, moon, and planets circumnavigate the center of the Milky Way every 250 million years.

Currently, earth is home to billions of people.

One of them is you. Another is me.

> I have no idea how
> small I really am. Or
> how big God truly is.

Speaking of you and me, here we sit, reading these tiny printed characters on this page. Along with you and me, there are over seven billion other humans dotting this little ball we call earth (our planet is a mere eight thousand miles in diameter), which is orbiting an average-sized star in a tiny solar system that's hovering on the outskirts of the Milky Way, one of billions of galaxies in the known universe, the size of which is always subject to upward revision with each advancement of measuring capabilities.

Again, a shrinking feeling is coming over me—like that day

in St. Paul's Cathedral—and I'm starting to clue in on the fact that I have no idea how small I really am.

Or how big God truly is.

Light flies, yet the universe that so easily blows our minds is nothing more than a speck to God. Scripture tells us,

> By the word of the LORD were the heavens made,
>> their starry host by the breath of his mouth....
> He spoke, and it came to be;
>> he commanded, and it stood firm.[2]

In other words, God created the cosmos without lifting a finger. And when He created the heavens, He did it all without the aid of a "How to Make a Universe" kit, an existing photo, a template, or a diagram. God was creating in the truest sense of the word, speaking the world into existence out of absolutely nothing.

> He sits enthroned above the circle of the earth,
>> and its people are like grasshoppers [to Him].
> He stretches out the heavens like a canopy,
>> and spreads them out like a tent to live in.
> "To whom will you compare me?
>> Or who is my equal?" says the Holy One.
> Lift your eyes and look to the heavens:

Who created all these?
He who brings out the starry host one by one,
    and calls them each by name.
Because of his great power and mighty strength,
    not one of them is missing.[3]

God is more massive than our wildest imagination, bigger than the biggest words we have to describe Him. And He's doing just fine today—sustaining galaxies, holding every star in place, stewarding the seemingly chaotic events of earth to His conclusion within His great Story.

God is constant. He blinks and a lifetime comes and goes. To Him, "a day is like a thousand years, and a thousand years are like a day."[4] All of human history could be written on His fingernail, with plenty of room left over for more.

God has no dilemmas. No quandaries. No counselors. No shortages. No rivals. No fears. No cracks. No worries. He is self-existent, self-contained, self-perpetuated, self-powered, and self-aware. In other words, He's God and He knows it. He is timeless. Ageless. Changeless. Always.

After an eternity of being God, He shows no signs of wear and tear. He has no needs. His accounts are in the black. He's the Owner, not to mention Creator, of all the world's wealth and treasure. He made the gold and silver, and the trees we print our paper money on. He owns the cattle on a thousand hills, and all the hills the cows are standing on. He holds the patent on the skies above—not to mention the earth, the seas and their depths below, the breeze, the colors of the sunset, and every flowering thing. They all are His invention. His design. His idea.

> ## He is timeless. Ageless. Changeless. Always.

God does whatever He wants. His purposes are a sure thing. There's no stopping Him. No containing Him. No refuting Him. No cutting Him off at the pass. No short-circuiting His agenda. God is in control. He sends forth lightning from His storehouse. He breathes out the wind, waters the earth, raises up rulers, directs the course of nations, births life, ordains death, and, in the midst of it all, still has time to be intimately acquainted with the every-day affairs of everyone on the planet.

God knows everything about everything and everyone. His eyes race back and forth across the cosmos faster than we can scan the words on this page. There is not a bird flying through the air or perched on a branch that escapes His field of vision. He could start with Adam and name every man, woman, and child who has ever lived, describing every detail about each one. To Him, pitch darkness and midday are one and the same. Nothing is hidden from Him. He wrestles with no mysteries. He doesn't need to wait for a polygraph machine to decipher the truth. He sees clearly and comprehends all He sees. He has never known what it is to have a teacher, a role model, an advisor, a therapist, a loan officer, a coach, an adjuster, a doctor, or a mother.

God's rule and reign are unrivaled in history and eternity. He sits on an everlasting throne. His kingdom has no end. Little gods abound, but He alone made the heavens and the earth. God has never feared a power struggle or a hostile takeover. He doesn't have to watch His back. He has no equal. No peer. No competition.

It makes perfect sense that His name should be *I AM*.

And even more sense that my name is *I am not*.

You and I are tiny. Minuscule. Transient. Microscopic. A momentary and infinitesimal blip on the time line of the universe. A seemingly undetectable alliance of dust particles held together by the breath of God.

The sum of our days is like a vapor—our accumulated efforts like dust in the wind. Among us, even the richest of the rich owns nothing. The strongest of the strong can be felled in one faltering heartbeat. We are fleeting mortals. Frail flesh. Little specks. Phantoms.

If this fact makes you a tad bit uncomfortable, you're not alone. Invariably, when I talk about the vastness of God and the cosmos, someone will say, "You're making me feel bad about myself and making me feel really, really small," as if that's the worst thing that could happen. But the point is not to make you *feel* small, rather to help you see and embrace the reality that you *are* small. Really, really small.

But that's not where the Story ends.

Though we are transient dust particles in a universe that is expanding faster than the speed of light, the unexplainable mystery of mysteries is that *you and I are loved and prized by the God of all creation.*

Simply because He wanted to, He fashioned each of us in His own image, creating within us the capacity to know Him. And if that wasn't staggering enough, in spite of our foolishness and rebellious hearts, God has pursued us with relentless passion and patience, fully expressing to us His unfathomable love through the mercy and grace of the Cross of His Son, Jesus Christ.

Sure, just a glimpse of His glory instantly resizes us to microscopic proportions. But God is not trying to deflate us with a Milky Way–sized put-down that erodes any sense of self and reduces us to a pointless existence. Just the opposite. When we see how tiny we are, our self-worth and our God-given worth can become one and the same as we are stunned with the reality that we have been made in His very likeness and invited to know Him personally.

I am not but He knows my name.

I am not but He has pursued me in His love.

I am not but I have been purchased and redeemed.

I am not but I have been invited into the Story.

I am not but I know the Creator of the universe.

I am not but I know I AM!

Let the depth and wonder of the words sink in.

I am not but I know I AM.

That's the complete Story—the entire gospel—the whole truth about who you are. You are small, but you can be on a first-name basis with *I AM*. You're beyond tiny, but if you are a believer in Jesus, every ounce of you has been bought and redeemed by God's Son. You are a galactic nobody—in fact, 99.9999999999999999 9999999999999999 percent of the people on earth have never heard of most of us. But God knows everything about you and calls you His own.

What more could we possibly achieve on earth that is greater than what we already have? We are already friends of God. What greater prize or position could we hope to gain? What praise from human beings could eclipse the voice of *I AM* speaking to us by name?

One of the joys of knowing our new name—of celebrating *I am not*—is that it allows you and me to bypass the all-too-familiar trap of thinking more highly of ourselves because of what we have accomplished or who we know. I'll never forget when that clicked for me.

I had just walked into a packed ballroom in Nashville during Gospel Music Week, where the who's who in Christian music had gathered for four days to network and honor the year's best with the GMA Dove Awards. The room was filled with artists, label heads, managers, booking agents, and just about anyone who was a somebody in the industry.

During the day, I kept noticing the elaborate name tags around everyone's neck. Marked with all kinds of special colored ribbons, the name tags were minibillboards, broadcasting to those in attendance just how important, or unimportant, each of us was. You could see it everywhere—people crammed in elevators and huddled in conversations, straining to catch a glimpse of the critical data printed on everyone's badge. *Is he a somebody? Should I speak to her? Don't look now, but that's so-and-so!*

But I wasn't there to just hang around. I had been invited to speak at the luncheon. My message for the day just so happened to be "I am not but I know I AM." I felt nervous—not only because I was a peon representing a label most people had never heard of at the time, but because I knew I'd been invited to bring encouraging words yet instead had arrived carrying a stake that God was asking each of us to drive through the heart of self.

Well, somewhere during the message, after we had established the fact that all our names are actually *I am not,* I suggested that the kind GMA folks could have saved a ton of money and streamlined the registration process by simply putting *I am not* on each name tag instead of our individual names. Not only would this simplify things, but also it would be much more accurate and remind us all that the mission of our industry is clear—making much of Jesus until the whole world hears His name and sees His fame.

What a concept! And what a way to walk through life, entering every environment with every intention to shine as little light as possible on me and as much light as possible on the Son of God.

Later, I was happy to see a guy in the hallway with a black mark through his name and the words *I am not* inscribed below. To complete the message, the guy really needed to add the rest of the phrase: *but I know I AM.* That's the name tag!

We know God—and He knows us too—inviting us to an intimate union made possible when He took an extraordinary step from the hugeness of heaven to the narrow streets of one small town on earth.

Became

The Church of the Annunciation sits off a crowded, narrow street in the heart of Nazareth, the town where Jesus grew up. The church is so named because it was in this little village that the angel appeared to Mary announcing the miracle birth of God's Son.

Inscribed in the stone facia high above the church's entrance are the words *"Verbo Caro Factum, est et Habitavit in Nobis."* Knowing little Latin, I leaned in to ask our guide for a translation.

"And the Word became flesh and dwelt among us," he said.

Of course, I thought.

Never did these words from the opening chapter of John's

gospel seem more fitting. Closing my eyes, I could almost hear little boys running through the streets as they laughed their way around another summer afternoon. This is where Jesus played. Where He grew. This place was the neighborhood of the Savior of the world.

Just slightly up a hill, at the end of a narrow, twisting alley, is the site of the synagogue where, on that fateful Sabbath, Jesus shocked the world. Taking in His hands the scroll for that day's prescribed reading, He proclaimed,

> The Spirit of the Lord is on me,
>> because he has anointed me
>> to preach good news to the poor.
> He has sent me to proclaim freedom for the prisoners
>> and recovery of sight for the blind,
> to release the oppressed,
>> to proclaim the year of the Lord's favor.[1]

The clincher, however, was His closing line: "Today this scripture is fulfilled in your hearing."[2] That's the claim that turned the religious world upside down. In fact, His claim to be the fulfillment of Isaiah's prophecy was tantamount to Him coming right out and saying He was the Messiah—the Anointed One of God—an unbelievable proposition to those who knew Him as Mary and Joseph's kid. In a heartbeat, pandemonium broke out and cries of "Blasphemy!" were on people's lips. The audience that

---

moments before had been listening intently was now a mob chasing Jesus to the edge of town, trying to hurl Him off a cliff.

So much for being the hometown hero.

I quickly grabbed my journal and copied the inscription from the top of the church. Below the Latin words, I wrote the verse in English and determined that for the next few days, I would meditate on the words one at a time. Using what I call "The One-Word Bible Study Method," I would let the verse sink into my heart and mind by contemplating each successive word for an entire day. (See Appendix A: "The One-Word Bible Study Method.")

So the next morning I wrote the word *And* at the top of the page in my journal, and my one-word-at-a-time journey through John 1:14, NKJV, began. What happened over the next few days astounded me, as words big and small opened God's redemptive heart right before my eyes.

My journey unfolded like this...

DAY 1: AND

Yep. *And.* It all started with a simple conjunction. Just three little characters. A throwaway word, right?

I know what you may be thinking: *There's no way I'm going to spend sixteen hours thinking about a conjunction. There's no possible way I'm going to spend an entire day meditating on the word* and.

That's what I was thinking too. But I determined to stick with *and,* even though I wanted to rush ahead to a more captivating and significant word.

And—the Word became flesh.

And.

Finally, after carrying around *and* in my heart for a good portion of the day, I saw it. Wow! Suddenly, *and* blew me away. In this verse, *and* is not just a simple conjunction. No way. *And* is a huge statement—God's way of saying, "All the stuff in the Old Testament up to now has been pretty amazing, right? Well, fasten your seat belts. There's a whole lot more coming."

It was at this point that *and* really started talking: "Remember the power of God displayed at the Red Sea? That was amazing, but that's not all there is. Remember the visible glory of God that descended over the temple, causing everyone to hit the deck? That was awesome, but there's a greater glory coming. Remember Daniel, David, Joshua, Rahab, and the other men and women of faith? They all performed wonders, but the Story doesn't stop with them. God is not finished. Stay tuned. The Son of God is on the way. Messiah is coming here and now. God has so much more in store."

And.

For me, day one was full-on. I went to sleep that night convinced that I had only seen the tip of the iceberg of God's activity in my life and in the world around me. Given that I had seen God do so much in my lifetime, it made my mind race at hyperspeed to think of all that was still to come.

Who says reading the Bible is a drag? I was inspired by the hope unlocked by a tiny part of speech called *and*.

Encouraged, I moved on.

DAY 2: THE

Oh no, not again.

The, you may be thinking. *You spent a whole day meditating on the word* the?

Pretty deep, huh? I had progressed from a conjunction to a definite article. From *and* to *the*. Not exactly the stuff of devotional ecstasy, right?

I'll admit, I had my doubts too. But I went for it, anyway. And it paid off—big time.

Turns out, in this particular verse, the *the* is incredible, an integral component of what God is saying. You see, when God chose to do more *(and)*, He didn't just do something, anything. God did a very specific thing, a "you're-not-going-to-believe-what-I'm-about-to-do-now" thing. God sent His Son, the living Word, into a frantic Bethlehem night in the form of a baby, into the streets of Nazareth in the frame of a little boy.

And Jesus wasn't one of many sons; He was *the* only Son. He wasn't one of a multitude of messengers sent from above; He was *the* Message and Messenger come down from heaven to earth.

God did one thing.

He sent one Son to be the Way.

John doesn't write that *a* Word became flesh.

Or that *some* Word became flesh.

Or that *the flavor-of-the-day* Word became flesh.

Or that *a really good* Word became flesh.

And certainly not that *one of many* Words became flesh.

John carefully wrote *the* Word. The one Word. The definitive Word. The one and only Word—Jesus Christ.

> The one Word. The definitive Word. The one and only Word—Jesus Christ.

On day two I fell in love with *the,* because *the* was all about the uniqueness of the Christ, the full and final revelation of God to humankind.

Day two was a wonderful, faith-strengthening, worship-evoking, gospel-underscoring day.

DAY 3: WORD

This day was all about the big-*W Word,* not the small-*w* one. The latter is all about the vocabulary of human beings, but the big, capital-*W Word* is all about the language of God. Day three was a celebration of Jesus, the One who embodied everything God wanted to communicate to the whole wide world. Once again, after four hundred years of silence, God was talking, and Jesus was His one-Word proclamation to all who would listen.

Jesus was not just clever at crafting words; He was *the Word.* He wasn't just the best sermon giver who ever lived; He was the Sermon itself in all its fullness. In the end, what mattered wasn't just embracing what Jesus was saying, but embracing the One saying it. For everything God was, and ever wanted to say, was embodied in the person of Jesus Christ alone.

Well, I think you're getting the hang of it by now, so let's move on to...

DAY 4: BECAME

Honestly, I was still on overload from days one through three when I slowly penciled the word *became* in my journal. At first I thought *became* was going to fit more in the category of the words *the* and *and* in my one-word journey. But then God detonated the word *became* in my heart, obliterating the calm of a perfectly beautiful afternoon.

A breeze was blowing in from the Sea of Galilee toward the landscaped hillside—the place many claim to be the site where Jesus preached the Sermon on the Mount. Our group had scattered across the grounds of yet another sacred church to quietly reflect on His sermon's succinct words before heading back to our buses and moving on to another location.

I was sitting alone under a tree, staring at the word *became,* replaying the verse over and over in my mind. "And the Word *became* flesh and dwelt among us."

Became.

I let that word settle into my heart. And I waited.

And then, in the quiet shade, the word *became* leaped off the page and shot through my heart. I wanted to scream but couldn't for fear the nuns valiantly patrolling the grounds would expel me—not to mention that I'd ruin a perfectly peaceful moment for everyone else in our group.

But I could barely control myself. There it was, right in front of me. *Became.* The gospel in one word—redemption's story shrunk down to six amazing letters.

Do you see it? *Became* is a compound word, meaning it is comprised of two words—the word *be* and the word *came.*

Or simply, *BE.*

This verse is about Jesus, the One who bears the same name as the God who appeared to Moses at the burning bush. That day God revealed Himself to Moses as *I AM—I AM WHO I AM*— the present tense, active form of the verb *to be.*

Or simply, *BE.*

God told Moses that His name is *BE,* the very name Jesus used when He claimed, "Before Abraham was born, I am!"[3] Jesus's name is *I AM.* Jesus is *BE.* And *BE* is one of the two words in our compound word, *became.*

I AM NOT BUT I KNOW I AM

In an instant, *became* turned into *BE came,* and I wanted to shout for joy from the side of that hill.

Now the verse read, "And the Word—whose name is *BE*—came."

Hello!

Wake the world. Jesus came! *BE* came! *I AM* came! But in a most surprising form. Right here for all to see, the Lord of creation took on the dusty frame of a man. The great *I AM* became *I am not*—God spanning the gap to you and me in the person of His only Son.

BE came because you and I could never get to *BE* on our own.

BE came so that we would know that we matter to God.

BE came to give us life again.

BE came to rescue us from the small and fleeting stories of us.

BE came to make a way for us to join the never-ending Story of God.

BE came because He could.

BE came as a one-word summary of God's message of grace and mercy, the end of humanity's futile attempts at finding our way to Him, the deathblow to religious systems that attempt to lift us heavenward.

When *BE came,* it spelled the end of every way of thinking that we, even on our best of days, can attain the heights of the righteousness of God.

Our story is *not* that we can muster the strength to raise ourselves up. Rather, God has come down to us—Jesus, walking on planet earth. Here.

That, my friend, is simply astounding.

Day four was a day that forever changed my life, recasting what I have believed for most all my days into fresh and tangible skin…for how did *BE* come?

DAY 5: FLESH

BE came flesh. God arrived with skin, the Divine in the form of a sweaty, laughing little boy playing with other kids in a narrow street on a steamy afternoon.

That's how God chose to connect with us, to deliver us, to come for us.

God didn't send a note, an e-mail, a check, a cosmic event, a mandate, or a vague religious image on a toasted cheese sandwich. When God came to the human race—when *BE* came—*BE* became *flesh*. The God of the world in a body like yours and mine.

Why does it matter? Because you can touch flesh. You can identify with flesh. You can wrap your arms around flesh and feel its heartbeat. You can hear the voice of flesh and look into its eyes. And if you're searching for a sacrifice for the sins of all humankind, you can pierce flesh and it will bleed. You can nail flesh to a cross.

Day five was a reverent day—a celebration of divine incarnation, the staggering mystery of the fullness of God in bodily form.[4] Day five was a clear vision of the Father's unmistakable Son, standing full of grace with both feet firmly planted in our broken world.

I AM NOT BUT I KNOW I AM

What earth-shattering truth—*And the Word became flesh...*

But another conjunction was on the horizon, signaling that there was much more to come.

DAY 6: AND

Again.

It seems like it would be enough that God, after all He had done through eternity past and throughout the history of human-kind, sent us a living, breathing message straight from the throne of heaven. But there's more...

DAY 7: DWELT

It wasn't enough for Jesus to just make a splash across the head-lines with a well-timed photo op that would lead the evening news. No, Jesus didn't just "drop in"; He came to dwell with us.

Jesus, though far from His rightful throne, wasn't just a mo-mentary visitor to our tiny planet. He was, for thirty-three years, a resident of earth. His wasn't a fleeting flyover but a daily grind, one that put Him in touch with the ins and outs of our struggles and pain.

Jesus lived. He laughed. He played practical jokes like kids are prone to do. He got tired. Was frustrated. He ate. Swam the lake (and at times walked on it). Soaked in the beauty of the sunset. Played with the neighbor's dog. And rarely missed a chance to hang out at a party or dinner. He felt isolation. At times, raised

His voice. Jesus knew what it was like to share a quiet meal with close friends.

Yet, all the while, Jesus was not like the others. He knew who He was and what He'd come to do.

As I stared intently into the word *dwell,* it quickly became apparent that the bulk of this little gem is the word *well.* And that's what was on Jesus's mind as He walked and talked among us. Jesus came to make things new, to make us whole again.

DAY 8: AMONG

Jesus wasn't shy about mixing with people. Whether they were rich or poor, He was equally quick to invite Himself into their world. Whether people were high or low, religious or scorned, Jesus would slip up beside them and look into their eyes. Almost without a word, He would transfer value, a love like no other. And He offered grace to all who were thirsty for more than this world could give.

Nothing says it better than Eugene Peterson's rendition of John 1:14 in *The Message:* "The Word became flesh and blood, and moved into the neighborhood."

Jesus truly was the people's King.

A friend of sinners.

Relevant before relevant was cool.

Emmanuel.

God with (and among) us.

DAY 9: US

Wow!

Day nine was a beauty!

Right there, smack in the middle of a grand story about what the Father had done, sat you and me. Us!

As it turns out, God's self-awareness (or God-awareness)—the fact that He is God, knows He's God, has always been God, and does everything for His glory—doesn't make Him indifferent to you and me. Rather, it was His plan all along to dwell among us.

Your name may be *I am not*, but you are not inconsequential to the Almighty. He loves you more than you could dream or imagine. I know there are days and circumstances that may seem to shroud the reality of His great love, along with feelings of your own (and, at times, the opinions of others) that assail His affection for you. But God's passion to connect your heart to His, and the extraordinary lengths He was willing to go to in demonstrating His love for us, are not mythic legend. On the contrary, history is split in two by a breathtaking journey—Jesus coming for us, the great *I AM* on a rescue mission of love.

The Journey

Recently, while attending a conference in Washington, DC, just a few blocks away from the White House, I was staying for several nights in a hotel that was even closer. In fact, as the crow flies, I was lodging about as close to the White House as possible without actually sleeping in the Lincoln Bedroom.

My hotel room was situated on an eighth-floor corner, with windows facing the Washington Monument and the Treasury Building. Just beyond, on the opposite side of the Treasury, I could see the building that housed our nation's most powerful office as well as the president and his family.

During the afternoon break, I was back at the hotel and headed to the business center on the second floor. As the elevator doors opened, I was met by what appeared to be a Secret Service agent, our eyes meeting for an instant before I said hello and nervously made my way around the corner, following the signs to my destination. Ever the curious one, and infused with a vivid imagination, I began to wonder who was in the hotel and for what purpose.

Once I was finished in the business center, I made my way back to the elevator bank, which sat on a narrow strip of floor that overlooked the open lobby below. The mood was definitely tense, and something important was up. As I looked down the corridor past the elevators, a heavy black drape was being hung and people were scurrying in and out of what I presumed was a ballroom or meeting room.

By now, there were two agents hanging out by the elevators, both eyeing me with undue suspicion. Their body language seemed to be saying, "It would be best for you to head back to your room."

But, not being one to miss out on any action, I pressed the button for the lobby on the panel of buttons inside the elevator and headed down. Once the doors opened, I knew my hunch was right. Secret Service agents were all over the place—a dozen of them, possibly more. *Maybe the vice president or a head of state is in the building,* I surmised.

I tried to act nonchalant (something my wife tells me I'm not good at) and steadily walked past the check-in desks toward one of the two main lobby entrances. Soon, an agent engaged me and asked if he could help me. Quick on my feet, I said I was hoping to use the hotel's ATM machine around the corner of the lobby (which, at some point, I actually did need to do).

"I'm sorry, that won't be possible," he responded.

"Um, okay, then can you tell me when it will be available?"

"Not anytime soon" was his reply. "This area won't be accessible for several hours."

Several hours? What in the world was going down in *my* hotel?

Back in my room, I worked for a bit, caught up on e-mail, and got ready to meet friends at a restaurant next-door for an early dinner we had planned. That's when things got really interesting.

Looking out my window, I was startled to see two SWAT members on the roof of the Treasury Building across the street. They were both looking through the biggest binoculars I had ever seen, and one of them seemed to be looking right at me.

Uh-oh, I thought. *He sees me and has probably been tipped off that I was the guy on the second floor and in the lobby poking around to see what was going on.* I imagined he was saying into his radio, "I've got a read on the sneaky guy. He's in the southwest corner room on the eighth floor!"

I freaked out, moved away from the window, and proceeded to act like I was minding my own business and getting ready for dinner, oblivious to the fact that there was a heavily armed person in full SWAT gear standing eye to eye with me on the rooftop of the building across the street peering into my room with high-powered binoculars!

Looking out the other corner window, I could now see that the sidewalks had been lined with yellow caution tape and DC police were stationed all along the way and at every intersection. I

I AM NOT BUT I KNOW I AM

waited as long as I could to see what the fuss was about, but my dinner appointment was getting closer, so I headed out.

After arriving at the lobby level, I was met with the message that all guests must now leave the hotel from the floor below. That said, the doors closed and I, along with the other inquisitive guests who filled an elevator, were deposited one level down and ushered out a side entrance past a temporary metal detector that was being used to scan everyone entering the property.

Once outside the door, I ran into friends who were staying at the same hotel. Instead of going in, they were camped on the sidewalk waiting to see what was about to unfold. "Rumor has it," they reported, "the president is coming to *our* hotel."

I'll spare you the rest of the minutia, but within a minute or two, the sound of a motorcade could be heard a few blocks away. Every police officer, Secret Service agent, and security type in sight immediately went into "go mode" as several motorcycle police roared past.

Soon a half-dozen black SUVs streaked by, then two presidential limos, one empty, the other carrying the POTUS—the president of the United States. Yep, I saw him as plain as day.

Slowly, both limos, closely followed by several emergency vehicles, a press platoon, and additional black cars and more police, made the turn at the opposite corner of the hotel and disappeared into a makeshift tent that filled the street and shrouded the limos once they stopped at the hotel's door.

I wasn't sure why, but the president was on the move. His destination—the place that I temporarily called home.

After the long and circuitous walk I now had to make around several blocks in the opposite direction, I arrived at the restaurant for a quick bite with friends and fully recounted the story. When I returned to my hotel, several hours later, it was as if nothing had happened. By now, all was clear and things were back to normal. There were no agents, no fanfare, no crowds lining the streets. I could even use the ATM machine.

Back in my room, I went online and pulled up the president's published daily schedule. There it was—at 5:15 p.m. that afternoon, the leader of the free world had a campaign fund-raising event in our hotel. At this point, I wish I'd had the presence of mind to check the schedule earlier while I was trying to figure out what was going on. But now I was intrigued and decided to check our location in Google Maps, gauging the distance from the West Wing door of the White House to my hotel. Using the little mile/meter measurement in the corner of the map, I traced his journey. So, how far did the president travel? Roughly fifteen hundred feet (a little less than five hundred meters).

Smiling, I was thinking what it must be like to be in a position so great that it required such massive and intricate preparation and execution to travel to meet some people for a reception that was literally across the street.

Pretty soon my mind drifted to Jesus—*the Word became flesh and dwelt among us.* I started thinking about the trip He made, the distance He spanned, and the cost required for Him to come from heaven to earth.

I started thinking about the day He said yes to the Father's rescue plan and how that one decision set off a domino effect that shaped and guided every subsequent second of history. I tried, though in vain, to think about the caravan of angels that escorted His arrival and the toll He paid to bridge the gap from His royal throne to a simple stable.

Honestly, I don't think it's possible this side of heaven to fully comprehend the staggering sacrifice required for the Creator to take on the form of the creature and settle in the neighborhood. But I know it's a lot—more than all the cash and treasure our world contains. And I know it says something profound about us little earth dwellers, whose names are *I am not.*

Just because you are small, never confuse that with being insignificant to God. Coming face to face with your humble estate doesn't nullify the love that drove the Son to give His all for you. You are little. But you are intensely loved. You *are not,* but *I AM* thinks enough of you to organize a visit that divided history and forever defines your worth.

It's true that God is God-centered. How can He not be? But the God-centered God has His eye on you. Scripture and history bear out that God does all things for His glory. And one glorious thing He has done is to gloriously fashion you and choose you in His relentless love. Thank God He did! For unlike the president's fifteen-hundred-foot journey, the gulf Jesus bridged for us is the distance from God's holiness to our sinfulness, from His majesty to our mess.

I think most of us, given the motivation and effort, could

make it from my hotel to the West Wing of the White House. But none of us, even with heroic motivation and effort, can make it to the righteous throne of God. The reason is clear: Sin doesn't make us bad; sin makes us dead.[1] And dead people can't travel even one inch toward God.

That's why Jesus's journey is so stunning. Not only is He the great *I AM,* Jesus—to show how amazing the Father's love is for each of us—came as the only one to ever be born alive without sin so that He could bring to life those who are dead and who could *never* do a thing to deserve or earn His love. In fact, Scripture says, "God, being rich in mercy, because of the great love with which he loved us, even when we were dead in our trespasses, made us alive together with Christ."

But that's not all. The passage goes on to say that He "seated us with him in the heavenly places in Christ Jesus, so that in the coming ages he might show the immeasurable riches of his grace in kindness toward us in Christ Jesus."[2]

Our lives, once awakened by grace to a glorious God, are to be pulled Christward in Spirit-powered transformation, the unworthy being welcomed by a supernatural visit from the King of the universe. In the end, the Story is about us—in that we were worth such a journey—but it's more about the One who made the excursion and the cost He willingly paid to touch down on our turf.

Our names may be *I am not,* but don't be confused:

You are loved.

You have been sent for.

You are prized.

You are His.

You have been sought out.

You are created and known by God.

You are chosen.

You are the apple of His eye.

You are made in His likeness.

You are not to be left behind.

You are valuable.

You are reachable.

You are rescue worthy.

You are worth the gift of His life.

You are made for His glory.

Rewinding to our "One-Word Bible Study Method," the next few words in John 1:14 continued to blow me away.

They read, "And we beheld His glory."

So let's continue and finish out the verse…

DAY 10: AND

Yes, another *and*. If it isn't enough that God wrapped Himself in human flesh and moved into the neighborhood, there's still more. *And…* Let this little game changer of a word settle in and define your faith right now. Wherever you are today, there is a flag emblazoned with the word *and* flying over your life. Sure, the past is real and its consequences are in some ways with us forever. But today is a new day. A new beginning. And God's mercies are new every single morning.

Don't keep looking back in fear that your story will be defined by either the successes or the failures of yesterday. Let hope rise and darkness tremble. God is the same yesterday, today, and forever. He's still working and you are still His. Your story is not finished. There's more to come. Turn the page. *And...*

DAY 11: WE

All of us. You and me. Each of us. None of us excluded. The good and bad of us. The great and small of us. The rich and poor of us. The near and far of us. The old and young of us. The most likable and most unlikable of us. The famous and obscure of us. Every one of us.

This message, this Jesus, has a broad reach. Trust me, if Jesus has already spanned the gulf from heaven to earth, He can make it all the way to where you are. The offer of Nazareth's miracle proclamation is not "Grace and truth for everyone else but you"; it's "Grace and truth for everyone and anyone who believes in Him." You're not too good to not need it—or too far gone to be excluded from it. *We...*

DAY 12: BEHELD

Hmm. I hope you're smiling by now and are already ahead of me on this one.

We *BE* held.

We *I AM* held.

How miraculous is that?

First, *BE* came, an unfathomable mystery in itself. But there's more: we *BE* held. We—little-bitty you and me—put our arms out to touch and hold the Son of God. Embracing Him. Holding on to Him. Squeezing to our chests the very Creator of the world.

And notice how the *BE* in *Be-held* goes both ways.

First, "we *BE* held," meaning tiny *I am nots* like you and me get to put our arms around the great *I AM.* But just as astonishing, we see that "*BE* held"—a beautiful picture of the God of the universe carefully wrapping His great arms of grace around you and me.

You are *BE* held.

Right now, whatever you're walking through, you are *BE* held. The arms that stretched out the universe like a curtain are wrapped around you.

On the day of Jesus's arrival on planet earth in the form of an innocent infant, Mary wrapped God's delivery in strips of cloth and held Him in her arms. But, as the Story unfolds, in time the tables turned—while hanging on the cross, her Son wrapped her in His words of comfort and hope.

BE came so that *BE* could hold. Yes, for a brief season, you held the Baby. But now and forevermore, the Baby is holding you.

DAY 13: HIS

His. What a centering and clarifying word. *His* is a possessive adjective. *His* is the counterpart to *my.*

This little powerhouse of a word takes us to the heart of the matter. The question becomes, "Who is going to take possession of our lives, our destinies, our day? Is today *His* or *mine*? Am I *His* or *mine*?" To "behold His glory" is to surrender *me* and *mine* to *Him* and *His.* For we can't take hold of Jesus without coming to terms with the fact that everything is already *His*!

I am His. My struggles are His. My future is His. My reputation is His. My needs are His. Everything is His!

DAY 14: GLORY

Glory, when you get right down to it, is what we all want. At least it's what our sin nature is constantly after. We want to be elevated. Recognized. Applauded. Noticed.

But, when Jesus appears and revelation occurs, all that ends. The fight is over. For we have seen *His glory*! And "Oh wow," there is no glory that compares to His.

How can we possibly demand to be pushed to the center once we glimpse Him? Why would we want all eyes on us once we have laid eyes on Him?

Jesus has true glory. He has the greatest worth. He has unfading fame. Jesus is significance defined. He is most beautiful. Splendid. Seriously stunning. Forever best.

Have you truly seen His glory? Have you truly seen Jesus?

The answer for you and me lies in the degree to which we are still promoting our own names and pumping up our own reputations. For when we come face to face with true glory, the kind that shrivels earthly adornments with supersonic speed, we start saying our good-byes to a life of self-made fame. Why? Because we don't need it! We have already *beheld* another unique brand of glory that is far superior to any glory we could fashion on our own!

My one-word-at-a-time study of John 1:14 began at the Church of the Annunciation in Nazareth, when I glanced up to see a Latin phrase carved in stone: *Verbo Caro Factum, est et Habitavit in Nobis.* In English, nine amazing words: "And the Word became flesh and dwelt among us." To which I added the next equally amazing five: "And we beheld his glory."

On that trip to Israel, I beheld with my own eyes not only Nazareth but also Bethlehem and Calvary—spots on earth that recount the story of Jesus becoming small so that we could see and know God's great glory. Each of them are real places that show us that life is not about us straining to be bigger than we are but about embracing the Christ-bought wonder in our smallness as we confess, *I am not...but I know I AM.*

I've made it to Nazareth a few times now, and once I get my bearings, I can find on my own the sites of the church and the nearby early synagogue where Jesus preached.

If only it were that easy to walk up and see the Story of God.

God's Passion for God's Glory

(and why God is not an egotist)

All this talk about God promoting His own glory can be a little unsettling to the soul. After all, aren't the core virtues of the spiritual life humility, quietness, and an others-first approach? The notion that God requires—even demands—worship, adulation, praise, honor, and glory seems to fly in the face of everything Jesus fleshed out as He modeled the prophet Micah's beautiful reduction of what it means to live well: "To act justly and to love mercy and to walk humbly with your God."[1]

And honestly, there's little in life we loathe more than people who strut around blowing their own horn. Seriously. Who wants to be around someone who is convinced that he or she is "all that," a self-absorbed, arrogant, self-promoting person who can't wait to seize any and every opportunity to push to the forefront and grab the spotlight?

So, how is it different with God? How is it that God can be so passionate about His glory and *not* be an egotist?

Before we take a stab at an answer, let's go back to the beginning of time as we know it. Scripture opens with ten clarifying words: "In the beginning God created the heavens and the earth."[2] Before we just cruise by this inaugural line, let's stop for a minute and let it sink in.

In the beginning God...

So, how did life and everything we hold dear come to be? God. What or who came first? God. Who thought up the universe and everything in it? God. Who was there before you or me or anything? God.

In the beginning God existed fully as God. In the beginning God was complete. Sufficient. Whole. Glorious. Worthy. Almighty. Perfect. Unique. In the very beginning God was the best of the best of the best.

And, as God, He had no shortages. No needs. No equal. No problems. The psalmist, giving us a glimpse into time-before-time, wrote,

Before the mountains were born
> or you brought forth the earth and the world,
> from everlasting to everlasting you are God.[3]

But that was just the beginning of time. God has existed unchanged forever. Having no beginning, God hails from eternity past—a concept that outstrips human understanding in the same way that it would tax an ant to explain the design and function of a laptop computer.

God has existed unchanged forever.

Before time, God perpetually lived in the presence of God—a beautiful triune deity (Father, Son, and Spirit) surrounding Himself with Himself in endless, brilliant, and utterly mind-blowing splendor. It's safe to say that in the beginning, and without beginning, God was doing just fine. Actually, more than fine. God was awesome before we ever heard or spoke His name.

Yet, even in this state of eternal, pre-beginning, before-time divine bliss, God had you in mind. That thought alone should cause you to drop this book in your lap and shake your head in amazement. In the beginning, and from the beginning (the beginning-which-had-no-beginning), Father, Son, and Spirit are thinking about how much they love you, and how they are going to create you beautifully (as you are) for the sole purpose of sharing an intimate and forever-long friendship with you. Think about it: the Divine crafting and pursuing a mere mortal, God reaching down to reveal Himself and His matchless glory to humankind.

Let this thunderclap of truth sink in: you were in the mind of God in eternity past. Yet, as God thought about you and me, His mission wasn't to point us to ourselves but rather to open our eyes to fully enjoy Him. From the start, God was intent on making sure we knew how truly magnificent He is.

Thus we can surmise that when God made the universe His goal, it was not simply to create a habitat for humanity but rather to make a statement about Himself. As He fashioned earth, God was not primarily acting as our interior (and exterior) designer, creating a global environment we would love and enjoy. No, God was thinking mostly about Himself.

In fact, if God were merely making a dwelling for humankind when He crafted the universe, He totally overshot His production quota. And this is a fact that baffles many within the scientific community as they try to reconcile the proposition that "God created" with the reality that everyone alive can easily fit on a teeny-tiny planet in an average-sized galaxy in the midst of a measureless (at least at this point in science's capacity) cosmos. If God was trying to make a place for us to live, didn't He end up with a lot of wasted space?

To this I respond, "Absolutely!" If the universe has as its chief function the accommodation of the human race, it's way too big. But what if creating a dwelling for you and me was not the primary variable that determined the size and scope of the universe?

What if forming our living quarters was only a minute fraction of what was going through God's mind when He spoke the world into existence? What if God was instead, as a matter of first importance, creating a universe that would reflect His expansive greatness, beauty, genius, and power? When you think about it this way, it turns out the universe is not oversized. It's just about the right size, after all.

Notice how calmly Genesis 1:16 describes, "God made two great lights—the greater light to govern the day and the lesser light to govern the night." And then it says with five concise words, "He also made the stars." Wow! That's not a bad thing to have "also" done. And when "He stretches out the heavens like a canopy, and spreads them out like a tent to live in," what is His motivation? Answer: "The heavens are telling of the glory of God."[4]

The stars, nebulae, quasars, comets, and dark matter do not exist solely to be objects of our astronomical pursuits. They exist to bring God praise. Their marching orders are clear:

> Praise him, sun and moon,
>> praise him, all you shining stars.
> Praise him, you highest heavens
>> and you waters above the skies.
> Let them praise the name of the LORD,
>> for he commanded and they were created.[5]

And the same is true of earth. When God initiated the first ocean wave and carved out earth's deepest canyons, when He opened the first flower and caused lightning to split the sky, each was a divine note in the symphony of His praise. When God was forming the very dirt we call home, and filling earth with astonishing beauty and variety, He intended that everything about it would echo His renown and point us back to Him. And when He created the first man and woman, God wasn't obsessed with the glory of the human race but with His own glory. Thus, God made us not in *our image* but in His—in the very likeness of a glorious Creator. As a result, His likeness is mysteriously woven into our DNA, the image-stamp of a glorious God, allowing us to share a unique intimacy with the Almighty and reflect His glory.

> ## God made us not in *our image* but in His.

Before there was time, God was surrounded by His glory. When God created, He did so out of His glory. As God fashioned you and me, He marked us with His glory. And so it is with all He does.

Everything God does, He does for His own glory. He approaches every decision with the question "What will bring the most attention and honor to My name in this situation—what will best put My glory on display?" Then He does whatever that is.

To put it another way, God is into God. God is highest in His own thoughts, foremost in His own affections. God doesn't love anybody more than Himself, exalts nothing above His own name, and does everything He does to the end of displaying His supremacy and luxurious wonder. That's why everything in all of creation is singing His song in this moment, and why the terminal confession of every human who has ever lived will be that "Jesus Christ is Lord." Why? The same verse tells us: "to the glory of God the Father."[6]

But if God does everything He does for His glory, does that make Him an egotist? Does the fact that He is bent on having all of creation bow down and worship Him make Him the world's biggest megalomaniac?

Well, if by the question we mean, "Is God full of Himself?" the answer is a resounding yes. Then again, if you're God, who else are you going to be full of? Hmm. Maybe you've never thought of it like that, but before we think less of God for thinking of Himself most, we need to consider His options.

By definition, God is the Sole Proprietor of the universe, the Originator of all that is, unchanging, eternal, and all-encompassing. Theologically speaking, He is omnipresent (everywhere at all times), omnipotent (all-powerful), and omniscient (all-knowing).

Therefore, one of the prerequisites of being God is that you know all things. So we ask, "Does God know who He is?" Does

He know He is supreme in every way—unmatched in glory, might, rule, and reign?

Well, if God doesn't know who He is, then by default He is not God. For to be God, and not know that You are God, would be proof that You were not who You claimed to be.

God knows who He is, stating clearly, "I am the LORD; that is my name! I will not give my glory to another or my praise to idols."[7] When He makes this confession (an assertion He is making not for His own sake but for ours), God is passing one test of being God, declaring that He knows full well who He is. God knows that He alone is God. He knows that He is supreme in eternity (something that we know, by the way, only because He told us), and He is fully aware of the fact that nothing, and no one, holds any value greater than His. God knows that He is intrinsically more valuable than all the worth of the world combined, and then some. And God is not just a little more valuable than the combined value of everything else in the universe that has value. He is *infinitely* more valuable!

In the end, all this self-knowledge of His superior value doesn't make God self-centered as much as it makes Him God-centered, something that He has to be because of who He is.

Are you with me?

Okay. So if God is God, and He knows who He is, God must perpetually exalt Himself in all things. For if God failed to exalt

Himself in every possible way, He would exalt something or someone else as central—someone or something that was not central at all. This would make God both unwise and unloving—unwise because it would demonstrate that He didn't know what was best, and unloving because He would allow our attention and affection to be aimed toward something that was less than the very best. But since God encompasses all wisdom, and is the source of pure love, He has no choice but to exalt Himself above all things.

If that approach sounds a little arrogant or egocentric, we have to remember who we're talking about. We're not talking about a little finite creature like you and me but about the God of gods who is before all things. If I make myself out to be central, or seek to exalt myself above all things, claiming that I am first or best, in that moment I become an egotist because I am neither of those things. I am not God and I know it. But when God orchestrates life in such a way as to spotlight His fame, He is being anything but arrogant. He is doing the most loving thing He can do. When He calls us to glorify Him—when He demands our complete and unadulterated worship—He is not being egotistical at all, rather He is simply being God. And He is doing the very best thing He could possibly do for us in that He is leading us to stake our claim on the most beautiful and glorious One in all creation. When God makes His glory the center of all things and the center of our affections, He is giving us Himself—the very best gift He could give and the ultimate expression of love.

Sadly, we are plagued with fickle tastes from the start. And as a result of the Fall, none of us make our choices out of pure objectivity, but rather we see dimly through a shattered lens and are driven by fleshly cravings that most often leave us busted and bruised on the side of the road.

As Scripture affirms, if left to our own choosing, we will without a doubt "trade down" and opt for less than His best.

Although they knew God, they neither glorified him as God nor gave thanks to him, but their thinking became futile and their foolish hearts were darkened. Although they claimed to be wise, they became fools and exchanged the glory of the immortal God for images made to look like mortal man and birds and animals and reptiles.…

They exchanged the truth of God for a lie, and worshiped and served created things rather than the Creator—who is forever praised.[8]

Yet God is tenacious when it comes to His glory. Whatever we try to do to replace it, He will use to amplify it even more. No matter how crazy the plot line of our sinful choices, God twists our turns into an occasion to show that He is better still.

If God is not an egotist, what does that make Him? According to the book of James, He is the giver of "every good and perfect gift…coming down from the Father of the heavenly lights."[9] That's exactly what happened when God gave Himself in the person of Jesus Christ. Except that on an eternal scale, Christ was *the* good and perfect gift, God's glory embodied for the world to see,

God's shout to awaken us from sinful slumber to look into His face.

If God is going to give us what is good and perfect, He must keep the spotlight on Himself. Thus God is determined that the Story remain about Him, ultimately concluding with the unending applause of heaven. His purposed preoccupation with His glory is a river no one can tame, a sovereign tide that overwhelms all our foolish pride. As He did with Pharaoh, so God will even use the greatest arrogance in human beings to amplify His glory, ensuring in the end that every life and every tongue affirms His fame.[10]

To joyfully choose to make our lives count for His renown is to join His cause and to get on board with what He is already doing with or without us. That way we make sure our lives count for what matters most while enjoying for all time the very best God has to offer.

Which is Himself.

Big River

It was a hot African morning when my wife, Shelley, and I, along with a small group of friends, finally made our way down what proved to be a treacherous descent into a gorge and to the Zambezi River below. If the trail that deposited us at the water's edge was any indication, we were already in over our heads, and we hadn't even gotten into the river. Upstream, we could hear the roar of Victoria Falls—the world's largest waterfall, cascading over rugged cliffs where Zambia and Zimbabwe collide.

After a few last-minute instructions from our guide, Steve, we strapped on our helmets, wedged into our raft, and drifted into the current.

Looking back on it now, I think we should have paid more attention to the dead hippopotamus ominously bloating in the morning sun as it floated in a nearby eddy. The hippo, Steve explained, had probably gotten swept away by the river's strong currents and hurled over the falls to its death.

Initially, the river was wide and inviting. We all had a good laugh at the first rapid when Steve purposely dumped us into the icy water. But as with the not-so-subtle message of the hippo, I should have considered Steve's words more carefully when he said, "You need to get used to being in the water. It's going to happen a lot today."

Getting wet wasn't such a big deal at first. In the water, out of the water—it all seemed like part of the adventure. Soon, though, the river narrowed, and the immense volume of water that flowed over the wide expanse of the falls began to squeeze into a narrow channel. As it cut its way between towering rocky cliffs, the mighty Zambezi created one Class IV rapid after another, and a few monstrous Class Vs. Fortunately, long stretches of quiet separated the rapids, but more and more, we spent the calm between series of the thundering white water dreading the inevitable.

As we drifted toward each successive rapid, the roar of the approaching turbulence increased. Steve would shout out paddling orders, then, working as hard as we could, we'd do our best to aim the raft into the rapid at just the right angle. Our two objectives: to stay in the raft and to come out safely on the other side.

At rapid after rapid, we failed, at least on the first objective.

No matter how determined we were to stay above the river, the waves would catapult the raft as if it were a tiny toy, sending bodies flying left and right into the raging waters. No matter how determined we were to hang on, each new rapid found us airborne and at the mercy of the currents.

By this time, all the laughing and joking had come to a stop and the panicking began, especially when we nearly lost a team member in the powerful current.

Thankfully, Steve led us to a walk-around on the last man-eating rapid (we were told this one was big enough to drag a school bus under), and we reached the midway point of the trip, where we were mercifully deposited alive and intact on a wide, sandy bank. This hadn't been one of our better days. Exhilarating, yes. Enjoyable, not so much.

And now we were faced with a choice. We could hike up and out, or we could carry on. While we thought it over, Steve informed us that the second leg of the journey was a lot more severe, with bigger rapids and, to add to the excitement, crocodiles sunning on the banks along the way.

Right there, our group took a vote. It was unanimous. We'd had enough. The Zambezi was too much for us. Our day was done. The river had won.

Not so visible, but much more dangerous, is the current that still flows out of Eden's garden. And guess what? We're all in it. More powerful than ten thousand Zambezis, the downstream effects of

Adam's sin still sweep us into the danger zone, that place where we're deceived into thinking and living as though we are bigger than we truly are.

Call it River Pride, white water that provides a thrill a minute while deluding us into believing we're in control. Just when we think we're riding the river, we find out the river is riding us, hurling us overboard at will and sucking us under.

It all started so well for Adam.

For proof, we don't have to even look past earth's first human. Although he had it all, the temptation to be as big as God was irresistible, and Adam stumbled and fell. When he sinned, he opened the floodgate of death and deception that robbed him, and us, of the joy that God intended.

It all started so well for Adam.

I mean, can you imagine waking up for the very first time to see the Creator of the universe staring back at you? Adam must have been floored. I wonder if the first words he heard were "Welcome! Welcome to the Story of God."

I don't know what was said that first morning, but I'm pretty sure Adam smiled back at God—once the gaping hole that was his mouth finally closed. After all, he was alone with God in a perfect world, drew his first breath from the Almighty, and was a living being uniquely wired for connectivity with the Divine.

Then Eve arrived, made like Adam in the image of God, and all was well in Eden.

But soon the world's first couple realized that the story unfolding around them was not about them. Instead, they had arrived on day six of a seven-day creation Story. And the Story already in motion was all about creating one—a grand epic in which God alone played the leading role. Yes, the two of them were invited to rule over the beasts of the field and were charged with populating the earth, but the whole world around them had been singing the Creator's praise long before they made an appearance on earth's stage.

The mood in paradise soured when Adam and Eve decided that their little supporting roles just weren't enough. They wanted a bigger stake. A higher profile. More of the limelight. They wanted to be as big as God.

Deceived, they believed the forbidden fruit was the ticket to the top, the one thing that would vault them to immortality.

But the fruit bit back, and Adam and Eve died, the first casualties of the pride that precedes every fall. Sadly, they didn't appreciate the fact that they were already immortal, carriers of the living breath of God. Sure, they were small, but they were living out their days *in* the Story of God. Yes, they were the first to bear the names *I am not,* but they were also the first to know the wonder of intimately knowing *I AM.* Now, in a heartbeat, their rebellion left them spiritually dead, abandoned to shrinking stories that would soon come to an end.

Do you see the point? When someone named *I am not* decides

to live as though his or her name is really *I AM,* one consequence always follows: we get swept away. Sooner or later, we end up like carcasses floating in the sun.

> We get swept away.
> Sooner or later, we
> end up like carcasses
> floating in the sun.

But let's not dwell on Adam and Eve. It doesn't take a magnifying glass to find the same temptation lurking within you and me. You'd think we'd learn from Eden's folly, but instead we seem more determined than ever to prove we're the exception to the rule, impervious to the current. We constantly thrust ourselves onto center stage, acting like life is ours to do with as we please—a drama that is all about me, myself, and mine.

And we're not the only ones. It's been that way in every generation.

Even after the Flood, human beings continued to think of themselves in glowing terms, grossly overestimating their position and power in the Story of God. After some time had passed, people said to one another, "Come, let's make bricks and bake them thoroughly.... Come, let us build ourselves a city, with a tower that reaches to the heavens, so that we may make a name for ourselves and not be scattered over the face of the whole earth."[1]

I'm not sure if they really believed God was only a few flights up or if they were just sold on their ability to build a tower into eternity. One thing I do know—they were squarely in the current of the Fall, once again seeking to make a name for themselves, when all the while, they already had one. But I guess building a memorial to the name *I am not* was not nearly glamorous enough.

Apparently, that's still the case today, wouldn't you say?

Things go terribly wrong when we try to assume control of our lives and those around us. For one, we sentence ourselves to bear a load (we call it the weight of the world) that God never intended for us to carry. Running our world is too much for us, no matter how hard we try. To try to be God—something I find I am really bad at—without having the wisdom and power of God is a ridiculous proposition, a daunting task. Attempting to orchestrate the world around us, even for a day, leaves us stressed and spent.

But there's an even greater downside to spending our lives making ourselves out to be bigger than we are. The danger is that we might succeed, at least in earthly terms, in making a name for ourselves. We might draw a crowd, grab some fame, amass some riches, hear the roar of applause. We might succeed at building a tower to the sky with our name emblazoned on it. All that hard work, only to have the River Pride deposit us on a sand bar called "The End." And in that moment, when the tiny story of us comes to a close, all the glory we could garner for ourselves will fade into oblivion.

Fortunately, there's another way to spend our lives.

If you've ever been in really big currents, you know it's pointless to try to swim against them. It's no different with the River Pride that's pulsing out of Eden. It's the most destructive current of all. Left to ourselves, we could never swim to safety. Even with our greatest effort, we cannot escape its power.

> Fortunately, there's another way to spend our lives.

The good news is that we don't have to. We're invited to accept, as a free gift, rescue from sin's deadly flow and a place in God's eternal glory—a place we don't deserve, but one He offers to let us share in through the death of His Son. The one requirement is that we trade the starring role in the miserably small stories of us for supporting roles in the great Story of God.

How?

Jesus became—*BE came*—small so that we could reach our highest and fullest potential in Him. He came down to lift us up out of microscopic stories that only get swallowed up in the grave, to place us in the river of His life that leads us home. He gave Himself for us so that we could die to self-fame, self-glory, self-effort, self-centeredness, and the self-stories that are quickly coming to an end.

I like to call it *glorious death*—our giving up our lives for something far greater. That's exactly what Jesus did, and what we, too, are called to do with our lives.

Your attitude should be the same as that of Christ Jesus:

Who, being in very nature God,
    did not consider equality with God something
        to be grasped,
but made himself nothing,
    taking the very nature of a servant,
    being made in human likeness.
And being found in appearance as a man,
    he humbled himself
    and became obedient to death—even death on a cross!
Therefore God exalted him to the highest place
    and gave him the name that is above every name,
that at the name of Jesus every knee should bow,
    in heaven and on earth and under the earth,
and every tongue confess that Jesus Christ is Lord,
    to the glory of God the Father.[2]

Jesus's death is the epitome of "glorious death"—death that leads to glorious and never-ending life.

In the same way, when we come to the end of ourselves, we're suddenly ready for God to do in and through us what we could never do on our own. His life and power bring the possibility of the supernatural activity of God to little *I am nots* like you and me. Not only do we know *I AM* but also *I AM* lives in us. He displays His power in us and glorifies His name through us. And in so doing we stake our claim in immortality, sowing our lives for His renown, investing in the applause of heaven that never, ever ends.

I'm not sure I'm going down the Zambezi again, even if I have the chance. But I'm positive today that I don't have to be swept away by the current of deception. What about you? Are you feeling the exhilaration of being on top of the wave? Or are you feeling the undertow dragging you down?

> ## Are you feeling the under-
> ## tow dragging you down?

The truth is, we become free of sin's power and disentangled from its curse when we die to pride and self, and we live instead in the powerful current of Christ's life in us—His eternal kind of life that's flowing in the veins of all who put their trust in Him.

The Little Leader

Nobody likes coming in second, third—or worse. No, something in us wants to always be on top, and somewhere deep within we quietly rejoice when our competition hits a snag or collapses.

Nowhere is this human tendency more apparent than when we're called to lead. Leaders must take a special responsibility for defining and reaching success (usually that means coming in first). You might find yourself in the leadership spotlight on a team or in a small group, in business, sports, music, or ministry. But wherever you are in a leadership role, prepare to get hit hard and fast by the impulse to be the biggest and finish first.

I imagine John's coworkers were in hyperventilation mode as they arrived with the news that his operation—and theirs—was no longer the biggest shop around. It appears the disciples of Jesus had taken up baptizing—in the same river, no less—and were drawing crowds that dwarfed those that were still coming to John.

You see, John was the first guy in the baptism business. Thus the name we still know him by today—John the Baptist. Technically, he was the *first* Baptist. Like me, you may have grown up going to the First Baptist Church in your town. But let's face it, John had the real thing—the very first Baptist church. A forerunner to Jesus Christ, John preached the good news of the coming Messiah, urging people to repent and prepare the way for the Lord. Soon, crowds were flocking to hear him teach, and people were being baptized in the waters of the Jordan River. In time, his reputation reached the Jewish religious leaders in Jerusalem and, curious, they dispatched some priests to investigate.

The political and religious climate in those days was tense. Four hundred years had passed since any visible sign of God's activity—four centuries of silence without any prophet, any voice. The entire Jewish world was on edge, suppressed by the Roman Empire, but on the lookout for anything that might signal the arrival of the Messiah, the Anointed One of God. Now John was pulling in huge revival crowds out by the Jordan River, and the Jewish leaders went to check things out.

Being in ministry most of my life, I can imagine how I might

I AM NOT BUT I KNOW I AM

have felt if my operation had grown so much that it caught the attention of the big dogs at headquarters and they had come down to see firsthand what was going on. Arriving on the crowded scene, the priests approached John and asked, "Who are you?"[1]

If there was ever a moment to stand in the spotlight, this was it. If there was ever an opportunity for John to take credit, snag some glory, and grab the headlines, the moment had come. There he was, a simple prophet, surrounded by devoted followers and some of the top religious leaders of the day. "How'd you build such a big ministry?" they began. "What's the key to your baptizing success?" "What do you have to say for yourself?"

> ## If there was ever a moment to stand in the spotlight, this was it.

But John knew exactly what (actually who) they were looking for. And he knew what he had come to do. So when asked about his identity, when given the chance to take center stage, John "did not fail to confess, but confessed freely, 'I am not the Christ.'"[2]

Notice the double use of the same phrase in his answer. John *did not fail to confess, but confessed freely,* "I am not the Christ." In other words, when it came time to either be the star of the show or shine the light on Someone else, John immediately directed the attention to the One he was called to serve.

And did you catch his opening five words: *I am not* the Christ.

Amazing! John seemed to know his name was *I am not*. (You may have thought I was making this whole "My name is *I am not*" thing up.)

They asked again, "Then who are you? Are you Elijah?"

John said, "I am not."

They persisted. "Are you the Prophet?"

He answered, "No."

Finally they said, "Who are you? Give us an answer to take back to those who sent us. What do you say about yourself?"[3]

Taking a deep breath (and having already clearly stated his *I am not* identity), John answered them in the words of the prophet Isaiah: "I am the voice of one calling in the desert, 'Make straight the way for the Lord.'"

The Pharisees shot back, "Why then do you baptize if you are not the Christ, nor Elijah, nor the Prophet?"

"'I baptize with water,' John replied, 'but among you stands one you do not know. He is the one who comes after me, the thongs of whose sandals *I am not* worthy to untie.'"[4]

It's as if John were saying, "Oh, I know you're looking for the Savior of Israel, but that's not me, even though it looks like we have a pretty major enterprise going on here and a ton of followers. I wouldn't dare take one iota of His attention or glory in this moment, because I know who He is and who I am not. You're looking for the Christ, but I am not He. I am just one little voice in the drama, one small mouthpiece crying out in the midst of a barren land, saying, 'Get ready, Messiah is coming.' I'm just a man.

"Yet, the One whose coming I announce is Holy God. He's

everything. And though I prepare the way for His arrival and baptize in His name, I'm not worthy to even hold His shoes at the door. Please don't mistake me for Him. My name is *I am not.* You're looking for *I AM.*"

The next day John was again baptizing in the Jordan when he saw Jesus coming toward him. I imagine his heart was now firmly lodged in his throat, but John managed to shout for all to hear, "Behold, the Lamb of God who takes away the sin of the world!"[5]

John knew who Jesus was, and when the moment arrived, he turned, pointed his finger, and exclaimed, "There He is"—or as we have in some translations, "Behold."

I know *behold* is an outdated word in our culture (if you don't believe me, just try to work it into a conversation or two today). But think about it with me. In the spirit of our One-Word Bible Study Method, *behold* can be understood as a one-word summary of what Christ's appearing was all about.

BE hold. *I AM* hold.

Jesus's very presence on the banks of the Jordan that day was God's proclamation that He wanted to wrap His Holy arms around us all—an invitation for us to reach out and take hold of Him. Like in the case of "we *BE* held," "behold" suggests the mysterious possibility that each of us can find our place in the eternal embrace of the God of the whole wide world.

And how was it going to happen? Because the Lamb of God was now stepping into redemption's story, taking on the sin of every human who would ever live. *BE* was going to be able to hold us—and invite us to cling to Him—through the sacrifice of Jesus Christ and the gift of grace He would offer to all people.

BE hold. *I AM* hold.

"Behold!" John cried. "There's the One we've all been waiting for!" Every head turned to look at Jesus Christ, the eyes of an entire crowd now riveted on one man. But scan the crowd and see if you can find John. Just a sentence ago, all eyes were on him. All the attention was his. People hung on his every word. Now he was out of the spotlight, just another face in the crowd with his eyes glued on Jesus.

And John seems so content, and even genuinely thrilled, to point people away from himself to one he believed was greater. As the crowd locked its gaze on the Christ, he continued, "This is the one I meant when I said, 'A man who comes after me has surpassed me because he was before me.'"[6]

I don't know about you, but that verse makes my head spin. John knew that even though Jesus came after him chronologically, He was already in the Story before him. Jesus may have just arrived in the area, but His name was *I AM,* meaning He had existed forever. From this, John deduced correctly that since Jesus existed long before he ever baptized the first person, Jesus was far greater than he could ever hope to be. John never thought his ministry outfit was number one, because the very One his ministry was about had already far surpassed anything he would ever do.

Like John, "little leaders" know who comes first in the Story. When they do accomplish great things or taste success, they do so with the realization that God had been on the scene for a long, long time and that He is the source of their vision, gifting, opportunity, creativity, energy, and breath. (No matter where we finish among human beings, Christ already has a permanent hold on first place.)

That's why John was never happier than on the day all eyes turned to Jesus.

If you don't believe it, notice what happened the next day. John was talking to two of his disciples (for "his disciples," you could insert "his team," "his key staff," "his church members," or "the guys he had poured his life into") when he saw Jesus walking by. The implication from the gospel account is that John's guys didn't see Jesus right away and might not see Him at all.

So, what's going to happen? Sure, yesterday Jesus had His moment to shine, but you have to wonder what might have been going through John's mind now. Was it *Oh no, not Him again*? Or *Hey, He got His props yesterday; let's get the focus back on me today*?

Nope. Once again, John announced for all to hear, "Behold, the Lamb of God!"[7] John wanted *everyone* to see Him. That's why he shouted, "There He goes again!" John went way beyond the calculated and polite response of giving Jesus the platform for a day—you know, that kind of false humility that somehow seems to telegraph its true intent no matter what we say. Instead, he showed his true colors as again and again he deflected the focus from himself to God. In fact, something in his voice (and eyes) was so sincere and convincing that two of his disciples turned and left him to follow Jesus.[8] Imagine that. Two guys you have invested in and led well, now turning away from you to follow someone else.

> ## John knew who he wasn't—*and who Jesus is.*

But that's what John was all about. John was a "little leader." I don't mean he was small in stature or vision or courage, or short on influence. Just that John knew who he wasn't—*and who Jesus is.*

There's something pretty powerful about knowing who you are—and knowing who you're not. Because John knew his name was *I am not,* he was free from:

- the seduction of fame
- the tyranny of comparison
- the delusional current of self-deception
- the never-ending scramble to the top of the heap
- ego
- jealousy

- backbiting
- a massively swollen head

And he was free from the ultimate ripoff—holding on to the starring role in a tiny story that was quickly vanishing from view.

No matter who you are, it's hard to stay on top forever, and it wasn't long until the new baptizer in town knocked John's operation from the top of the perch. At least that's what John's followers were spewing when they reported, "Rabbi, that man who was with you on the other side of the Jordan—the one you testified about—well, he is baptizing, and everyone is going to him."[9] Who was the new kid on the baptizing block? He was none other than Jesus Himself, and—surprise, surprise—everyone was going to Him.

There's nothing that gets under our skin or tests our motives more than the size of someone else's crowd, and John's team was raging with envy. After all, this Jesus fellow had come to them to be baptized in the first place, and for all they knew, He looked around, stole their ideas and methods, and then had the nerve to go right down the street and open up a baptizing operation of His own. Oh sure, even though *His* ministry was bigger, they could still stake their claim as "first." But for now they wanted John to fight back and take some kind of action against this idea-stealing newcomer.

But John knew his name was *I am not.*

In fact, he said it again for good measure. "A man can receive only what is given him from heaven. You yourselves can testify that I said, *'I am not* the Christ but am sent ahead of him.'"[10]

"He must become greater; I must become less."

He continued, "The bride belongs to the bridegroom. The friend who attends the bridegroom waits and listens for him, and is full of joy when he hears the bridegroom's voice. That joy is mine, and it is now complete." John was happy. His mission was accomplished, his role in the Story faithfully executed. The Groom had arrived, and John was the best man. *I am not but I know I AM.*

And then John uttered the words that pierce the flesh but free the soul: "He must become greater; I must become less."[11]

Let that phrase sink deep into your being: He must become greater, and I must become less.

John didn't politely say "He should increase." Or "I want Him to increase." Or even "It would be nice if He did increase." John's confession was not about tipping his hat to the Son of God. Rather, it was an expression of focused determination, a calculated purpose statement for life and ministry. It's as if John were saying, "No matter what else happens, there's one thing that has to take place— Jesus must emerge and expand in the hearts and affections of people. He must be elevated, honored, exalted, focused on, cherished, enjoyed, amplified, and adored by all people everywhere."

John's mission was simple and clear: Jesus must increase and I must decrease. Convinced that Jesus was center stage in the Story, John found great joy and compelling purpose in pointing others to Him. His is the voice of the "little leader," a man so blown away by the privilege of knowing God personally that he couldn't be distracted by petty clashes and glory wars.

Jesus was on a meteoric rise. In the short time since His baptism by John in the Jordan, Jesus had called disciples and established a core team, performed the first recorded miracle at a wedding up the road in Cana, and spoken to Nicodemus in the night about being born again, uttering the words of John 3:16—words that have become the most well known in Scripture. Jesus was clearly in a league of His own. But sadly, John's followers had been so busy trying to protect their turf that they had failed to notice that the kingdom had landed in the neighborhood. That kind of myopic, it's-all-about-me vision is the crippling by-product of not knowing who He is and who we are not, a truth John embraced and championed.

"The one who comes from above is above all," the gospel records, "The one who is from the earth belongs to the earth, and speaks as one from the earth. The one who comes from heaven is above all."[12]

In John's mind he wasn't losing his people to a bigger ministry. He was just doing what he came to do—holding wide the door for the arrival of heaven's King.

Be Still

Even God rests. That must have come as a huge shock to earth's original couple on the morning of day seven, their first full day on the job. After all, they had just arrived in God's creation Story and were now in charge of managing the garden God had made. Adam and Eve were together in love, a perfect match in a perfect world. They had no past, no baggage, no regrets, and no stress. Life was good.

That's why it's not hard to imagine their excitement when they awakened to their first full day on the planet. No doubt opening their eyes to the brilliant colors of the sunrise overloaded their senses and got their adrenaline pumping. The breeze, cool on their skin, carried a thousand glorious scents. The chorus of birds sounded like Beethoven to virgin ears. The man and woman were fully alive, armed with a vital mission and eager to get to work.

But just as they were penning their to-do list for the day, the voice of God rang out through Eden. "Good morning, guys. It's me, the Lord! Welcome to day seven. Everybody doing okay? I hope you had a great night's sleep and you're feeling good. Today is going to be a special day, an amazing day. It's your very first day here with Me, and you're going to love it."

So far so good, they were thinking. But then God's morning wake-up call took an unexpected turn. "I am not going to work today," He continued, "and I don't want you to either. Creation is complete. The universe is finished. Every star and each grain of sand is in place. The job is done. So let's just pause and drink it all in. Let's stop and consider what I have accomplished. Today we celebrate all that I have made. That means no work today, My friends. Today is a day of rest!"

"A day of rest?" I can hear Adam protesting. "But, Lord, we're not the slightest bit tired! We just got here, and we're ready to get busy doing what You have asked us to do. Why do we need to spend the whole day resting?"

I'm not sure if that's actually what Adam said, but I have a strong suspicion the questions raced through his mind. Here was a guy with a brand-new job to do, and the thing that made the least sense to him on day seven was rest. He and Eve hadn't even been alive for twenty-four hours. I mean, don't you at least have to *live* a full day before you can take a day off?

Adam and Eve were feeling fine. They weren't stressed out, overwhelmed, road weary, overworked, vacation starved, frazzled, worn down, bleary-eyed, overcommitted, or spent. Why would they possibly need a rest day this early in the game?

But maybe it was God who needed a break. After all, He was the One who had done all the creative work. Maybe He was the One who needed a rest. Right?

Wrong.

God wasn't the slightest bit tired on day seven. The Genesis account makes no reference to God sleeping or taking a break, or needing to. Making a world wasn't too much for Him. In fact, Genesis tells us that God simply spoke and the world came into being. In other words, He made the universe without so much as lifting a finger. It wasn't as if God had collapsed after six days of labor and needed a few more winks before getting started on a new day's work. No, God felt the same on day seven as He had before He invented time and space. On that day, He was just as omnipotent as He had always been.

So, if it wasn't exhaustion that caused God to take a break on day seven, what does it mean that He "rested" from all His work? I think it simply means that God paused.

And why did He pause? Because He's God and He works at whatever pace He desires. God has never had a boss, a supervisor, a deadline, an assignment, or a project due date. He does what He wants, when He wants. And after six days of creative genius, God stopped to celebrate all that He had done. He stepped back and took time to admire His efforts and to receive glory from all of creation.

So let's recap: On Eden's first Sabbath we find a man and a woman in perfect condition who have never known what it means to be tired. And we have a God who has known nothing but super-abundant energy for every second of His existence. Together, the three of them are ceasing from all labor to celebrate earth's inaugural day by...resting. Interesting.

Sabbath is funny like that.

You see, Sabbath is not so much about a day off as it is a "day up"—a day to remember that He is God and we are not. Without Sabbath, we forget who we are and lose sight of who He is, leaving us to carry the weight of the world on our shoulders. When there is no Sabbath in our lives, we become intoxicated by the lie that the sum of our lives depends on our effort alone. We get to the place where we truly believe that the outcome of the Story fully depends on us.

But in truth, we are tiny, limited beings. Our biggest and best efforts still accomplish far less than what God can do in us, through us—or without us—in one breath.

Enter Moses. Again.

Time has passed. Pharaoh has been defeated. Israel has been liberated by God's sovereign power. And once again, Moses is descending the same Mount Sinai where he had encountered the burning bush and heard his divine invitation.[1]

Talk about a mountaintop experience. Moses had been up

there alone on God's turf again. Mercifully, God had covered Moses by His hand in a crag in the rock while the back of God's glory passed by. Moses couldn't see God's face and live to tell about it, but trust me, he wasn't disappointed. He had nearly died from the brightness of the backside of God's glory. Coming down that mountainside, his face literally glowed.[2] But I think he was terrified—and thrilled to still be breathing.

This time, Moses carries down with him two stones inscribed by the very finger of *I AM*. Of the ten simple rules for godly living written there, one is a Sabbath command. It reads,

> Remember the Sabbath day, to keep it holy. Six days you shall labor, and do all your work, but the seventh day is a Sabbath to the LORD your God. On it you shall not do any work, you, or your son, or your daughter, your male servant, or your female servant, or your livestock, or the sojourner who is within your gates. For in six days the LORD made heaven and earth, the sea, and all that is in them, and rested on the seventh day. Therefore the LORD blessed the Sabbath day and made it holy.[3]

Obviously, all the commands are crucial (after all, there are only ten of them), but this one stands out because of the sheer volume of the words it contains. It's easily the longest of them all, comprised of ninety-eight words. Compare that to the last six commandments, which together total only seventy-nine words, and you get the feeling that God is trying to make a point. Apparently, Sabbath rest is not just a suggestion for the betterment of your life and mine but an essential, nonnegotiable command, an intrinsic part of the rhythm of life.

Clearly, Sabbath is about ceasing from labor, but at its core, Sabbath is about a whole lot more than sleeping in or catching a nap. Sabbath rest is about a state of mind, a deep-seated belief that God is the Creator and Sustainer of all things—an acknowledgment that He is sufficient and that He can be trusted. Because one of the symptoms of sin is short-term memory loss, we quickly forget that He set in motion the entire universe before we arrived on the scene. We need to get our memories corrected and our trust renewed by stopping long enough to remember that His name is *I AM* and our names are *I am not*.

In other words, God is holy.

The instructions Moses delivered require us to "remember the Sabbath day, to keep it holy." But what does it mean to keep the Sabbath holy? Well, the word *holy* conveys moral purity—and God is the very definition of pure—but the word also implies being set apart. When we say that God is holy, we are saying that He is not like any other thing. God is "other" (you could say He is completely unique—*uniquely* unique). He is unsurpassed in beauty and worth, forever and always the greatest thing in existence. There is no one like Him—never has been and never will be. In other words, God is holy.

If that's holy, and the Sabbath is supposed to be a holy day, then the Sabbath could be called "There's No One Like Our God" Day.

Or…

"God Is Not Like Anybody Else" Day

"I Am the Lord" Day.

"Make No Mistake About It—I Can Do Anything" Day

"Wow! Look What God Has Done!" Day

Or simply…

"I AM" Day.

To remember the Sabbath and to keep it holy is for us to say,

"Everything doesn't hinge on me."

"If I stop doing my part, the whole world will not fall apart."

"I am not in control."

"God made the world in six days without any input from me or my assistance."

"God doesn't need me to accomplish His work."

"I am little."

"God is huge."

"I trust Him."

I think that's what the psalmist had in mind when he wrote, "God is our refuge and strength, an ever-present help in trouble." And, "The LORD Almighty is with us; the God of Jacob is our fortress." But notice how the first-person voice of God emerges at the end of the song with a Sabbath call: "Be still, and know that I am God; I will be exalted among the nations, I will be exalted in the earth."[4]

> ## "Be still, and know
> ## that I am God."

Let's face it, stillness is not exactly easy to come by in today's culture. We are far more likely to be restless, anxious, fearful, fretful, and busy. But God's invitation is to be still—and to find again, in the calm pause, the assurance that He is, in fact, God. His plans are undeterred, and with or without us, He is going to receive glory from all peoples on the face of the earth.

But how do we find stillness when finances are tight, tragedy overwhelms, the kids seem out of control, nations are at war, relationships are strained, and there's just too much left to do at the end of the day?

It's simple. Still is found right next to *BE*.

See it?

"*BE* still, and know that *I AM* God."

That's right; the only place true stillness of the soul can be found on planet earth is in superclose proximity to the God of all creation. Sabbath rest is in His lap. Our inner calm waits within His embrace. Our peace of mind is found in the assurance that God is present wherever we are.

Like with Adam and Eve, we begin our mission on earth by doing nothing. Yep, *nothing.* We begin every day believing that God is already at work accomplishing His agenda, fulfilling His plans. We live each day like it was the very first day, a day that began at night, the time of day when we sleep and God works.

It's right there in the opening words of the Bible: "In the beginning God created the heavens and the earth. Now the earth was formless and empty, darkness was over the surface of the deep, and the Spirit of God was hovering over the waters."[5]

Day one began in absolute darkness, a place where no one could have worked even if they wanted to. "And God said, 'Let there be light,' and there was light. God saw that the light was good, and he separated the light from the darkness. God called the light 'day,' and the darkness he called 'night.' And there was evening, and there was morning—the first day."[6]

I'll have to admit that I didn't catch the day/night sequence on my own. I needed a little help from my friend John David Walt to notice that a day doesn't begin in the morning but at night. "And there was evening, and there was morning—the first day." In other words, night comes first, where darkness reigns, morning in the middle, and then daytime, which fades into night, where a new day begins again. That seems a little odd to us, and maybe even backward, but it makes perfect sense in the economy of God. John David said it like this: "We go to sleep, and God goes to work. And we wake up to see what God has done."

Oh, we still go to work when we wake up, but as we go, we

carry the spirit of Sabbath rest with us, believing that we have been invited into an already-in-progress Story in which God was doing just fine long before our little feet ever hit the floor.

It's a little like what happens when our favorite television show is interrupted by a late-breaking, "this just in" news story. After being transported halfway around the globe for some major development, or across town for a sensational car chase, we are sent on our way with the announcement "Now we join the regularly scheduled program already in progress." In an instant, we are whisked back to our show, but sadly we have missed some of the action and have to spend the next few minutes trying to figure out what happened while we were away.

In a way, that's the story of our lives. Everywhere we go, we walk into a story in motion. Before we ever arrive, God is on the scene carrying out His plan and causing all things to work for His fame. We arrive to join the regularly scheduled program already in progress.

So often we think that everything begins when we step through the door. We think the project happened because we had the brilliant idea, and we are convinced that the mission was accomplished because we chose to participate. But things don't start when *we* have a vision or *we* think of a new way of doing things, choose to act, have a burst of creative inspiration, give, or pray. God's Story is the already-in-motion story, a story that was happening just fine before we arrived and is going to go on just fine with or without you and me.

That's why we should wake up each day on the lookout for

the Story of God, constantly thinking to ourselves, *God is already here. What is He up to?*

I don't know about you, but I have to admit that practicing Sabbath has not been easy for me. I think that's partly because I was raised in a church culture and now live in a ministry world, which has often made Sunday the busiest of days. And it's partly because I have an inner drive that tends to push me past my limits. And it's partly—no, *all*—because I have a corrupted flesh steeped in sin that is determined to prove to the world that I can live life and accomplish great things on my own.

But the truth is, I can't do anything on my own. Every ounce of energy and each breath is a gift from God. And the life He requires of me—a life of goodness and godliness—is impossible for me to fully attain. I can't even keep those ten simple rules He gave Moses on the mountaintop.

Can you?

Fortunately, one of the great and mysterious joys of the Christian life is the reality of Christ's life within—a source of power and a quality of life that allows me to be all God calls me to be. That's why Paul wrote of a new mystery when he exclaimed that it is "Christ in you, the hope of glory."[7] He does not say it's Christ *and* you that brings the hope of a glorious life, but Christ *in* you. In other words, Sabbath is not about God and me operating as a dynamic duo. Sabbath rest is about me realizing that He is the only one capable of doing anything eternal in and through me.

That's the complete Story of the gospel—not just a better destination when we die, but a new power source within for every day that we live. To tap into that power source—the endless spring of Christ's life—is to experience Sabbath on a whole new level. That's the story of amazing grace, the hope of anybody in touch with just how small they are, and a truth I was reminded of one afternoon during a walk on an Alabama beach.

Furious Rest

I like to accomplish things. I like to dream, and often I see things that don't exist and try to figure out how to make them come to life. I like to build things and I'm into innovation and progress. I don't mind work. I respect productivity. But there's a downside. If I'm not careful, on the way to attempting something great for God's name, I can forget that mine is *I am not.*

That's where I was over a decade ago as I paced the shore on a southern Alabama beach. I was so caught up in my thoughts that I barely noticed the steady rhythm of the waves that were washing across my feet. In less than twenty-four hours, the meeting to end all meetings (or at least, so I thought) was going down. For me—

and the ministry of Passion Conferences—it was a pretty massive deal. On the table was the kind of opportunity that doesn't come along too often, and one that I never thought would be possible for us.

Two leaders from one of Christian music's most successful companies were on their way to meet with me at a beachside location where my family was on vacation. Yep, that's right—the big guys coming to me (insert first clue that I wasn't thinking straight). Within hours we would be across from one another, and I already knew what was going to be on the table. I would have one shot (just one chance, so I thought) to make our case. For me, it looked like a do-or-die moment (insert second clue).

So there I was, storming up and down the beach, rehearsing my presentation over and over, less than six feet from an ocean that stretched far beyond my sight. Yet I hardly noticed. Instead, I felt like a thousand-pound weight was strapped to my chest.

I frantically tried to tally everything associated with my life and ministry that could be considered strength. First, there were all the places I had spoken and the crowds I had stood in front of. Then there were the Passion gatherings and the CDs sold. We had a solid track record, not to mention future potential and the collected gifts and abilities of those on our team. Our upside seemed huge—and I was determined to squeeze every last ounce of persuasion out of it that I could (clues all over the place).

To put it straight, I was trying to impress these guys with our cause, hoping to convince them that a venture with our team was something they should pursue.

I wish I could tell you that I was at rest—that I was acting on the fact that everything was in the hands of God. Obviously I wasn't. I had been seduced into thinking that what happened the next day was pretty much all up to me.

Suddenly I sensed God's voice. "Why are you so perplexed by all of this?" He asked. "Why are you trying to make yourself seem so big and important? Louie, what you need to do before this meeting is to remember that you are really, really small."

Whoa, I thought. *Me? Small? Oh yeah, that's right! Okay, I'll be small. What a brilliant approach! What an amazing strategy! Tomorrow, when they show up, I'll go in with a superlow profile. I'll go in acting all small, and just when their defenses are down—wham!— I'll jump up and surprise them with our strength.*

What a great plan. "Thank You, Lord," I replied. "This is an incredible idea."

This time His voice seemed a little more firm. "No, Louie, you're not following Me here. I'm not saying you should go into the meeting acting small. I'm telling you that you *are* small."

Oh.

As those words bounced around in my heart, the truth finally started sinking in.

I *am* small. *Very small.*

After only a few more steps, my anxiety started to lift. Who was I kidding, anyway? As much as I may have wanted to believe otherwise, I was neither big nor important. And Passion, the ministry we had poured our lives into for years, was nothing more than a tiny cog in God's kingdom venture, an immeasurable enterprise that spans the globe and bridges generations. By comparison, Passion was small-time, and I was even smaller—just a little guy who has been chosen by God to play an incredibly small role in one little chapter of His expansive Story.

In a heartbeat, my game plan for the meeting changed. As I embraced the reality of my true size, a point that now seemed to be underscored by the countless grains of sand between my toes, the peace of God came rushing over me. Instantly, the weight was gone and I could breathe again. Instead of suffocating under the weight of thinking I was in control, I could now rest in the fact that God could do whatever He wanted with me—and I believed that He was going to do just that.

I didn't decide to skip out on the meeting or pass on the chance to make our case. I just settled into my new size and committed right there to open the meeting by confessing the truth about how small I really was.

Before long, I was sitting face to face with these two powerful music guys in a hotel suite. I was still a little nervous (okay, maybe a lot nervous), but it was the nervousness that naturally comes with being in a situation you've never been in before, not the other kind of nervousness that feels like heart-crushing pressure because we think the fate of the world is in our hands. It's a better kind of nervousness.

After the usual pleasantries and small talk, I said to them, "Before we begin, I just need to say something. When you get right down to it, I am very small and our team is really very small. We'd love to give this partnership a shot, but we are small-time players in God's kingdom Story."

A pretty persuasive opening line, huh? But with those words came rest. And the assurance that God is huge and completely capable of accomplishing His purposes for our lives.

Let's be honest, trying to be God is pretty heady stuff for humans. That's why each new week includes a day called Sabbath. And every day is to be filled with the attitude of Sabbath rest. But, remember, the current of self is deceptively strong. So strong, in fact, that Sunday is slowly being blurred into Monday, and nobody in the church or the world seems to care.

Trying to be God is pretty heady stuff for humans.

Well, nobody except the folks with the humorous cow commercials.

Growing up in Atlanta, I have always been partial to Chick-fil-A, a fast-food restaurant chain based here that enlists cows to help sell humans on eating chicken. Granted, I'm biased because my dad sketched the original Chick-fil-A logo back in 1964, and it's still in use today. I'm also a fan of their unrivaled chicken sandwich, addictive sweet tea, and homemade lemonade. But what I love most about Chick-fil-A is that they are closed on Sundays. Yep, lights out, bars down in the food court at the mall.

It's interesting that these guys don't seem to be losing any money. On the contrary, the company is expanding rapidly. But even if they were losing ground to their competition by being closed one day a week, would that be a bad thing? I think the folks at Chick-fil-A are doing exactly what God had in mind way back in the garden. They've created a great product (something it seems obvious to me that God followers in business should do), forged a memorable (and apparently effective) ad campaign, and worked really, really hard—creating great demand for their product and a loyal following. They have faithfully served the American consumer Monday through Saturday for over forty years. And on Sundays they've closed the doors and gone to worship, and in the process honored God not with busyness but with silence. Their unattended drive-through lines proclaim that they really do believe in the God who formed the universe without their help or anyone else's.

Some of us forget, though. On more than one occasion, Shelley and I have been out on a Sunday afternoon and, craving some Chick-fil-A sweet tea, pulled expectantly into a drive-through, only to wait at the order point for someone to talk to us from the little speaker box. There was even the time we honked impatiently. It took a while for us to look up and notice that we sat in a one-car line and there were no others cars in the parking lot.

Oh. It's the Sabbath.

But some of us forget more than just what day it is. We forget the simple truth of Sabbath rest, believing that the only way to stay on top is to work 365 days a year. Or worse, we take Sunday off but make sure the people who work for us keep our operation running seven days a week. We're afraid that if we stop working, we'll lose ground to the competition, give up market share, miss the deal, or fall behind the pack.

No, Sabbath rest is furious rest.

But I take you back to a chicken sandwich and sweet tea. These guys at Chick-fil-A have gained so much respect with consumers that mall managers will allow them to break ranks with other stores and shut their doors on the first day of the week.

How could you and I "remember the Sabbath day, to keep it holy"? Taking rest seriously doesn't mean laziness or lack of momentum. It's not a "Let's just sit back in the easy chair of life and let God do everything for us" rest. No, Sabbath rest is furious rest. It's the kind of rest that powers our journey as we follow Christ with every ounce of our energy.

Consider the life of Paul. In the days after Christ's resurrection and ascension, Paul was a hater of the Christian message and perhaps the number-one persecutor of the early church. He was on the fast track in the religious system of the day, with all the right credentials, education, and family ties. But a funny thing happened on his way to work one day. As Paul headed to a town called Damascus to oppress the followers of the Way, he met Jesus. Blinded by a bright light, Paul went from being a Christ persecutor to a Christ follower in one life-rearranging encounter.[1]

As it turns out, Paul would be God's choice to be the driving force behind the expansion of Christianity throughout the known world. Reading the rest of the story in the book of Acts, there's no doubt Paul was a Type-A personality. He was the sort who got things done, moving at a pace that would drop most of us in a matter of days. And on top of that, Paul faced physical hardship and persecution at every turn. But he never quit. In fact, he never even took his foot off the gas.

But Paul understood furious rest and penned the words "Christ in you, the hope of glory." He knew the secret of Christ's life within, a powerful engine of unstoppable strength that was greater than anything he could do on his own. That's why he went on to write, "For this purpose also I labor, striving according to His power, which mightily works within me."[2] Paul knew that rest and labor were not mutually exclusive, and he had no problem straining and striving to accomplish his mission. But Paul made it clear where the power came from.

That's what I call furious rest—giving all we have for the sake of God's fame, yet carrying Sabbath rest as we go, knowing that His life within us enables us to accomplish what He has called us to do.

Well, the meeting that day in Alabama went well. I now count those two business leaders as friends. For over a dozen years, we've been partnering to create music that will open people's eyes to the amazing Story of God that's going on all around them.

Not too long after that initial meeting, our team at Passion settled on the label name sixstepsrecords.[3] Then we set out to create a logo. We landed on a design comprised of six little dots in a spiral, tiny elliptical shapes that get progressively smaller. The idea behind the dots was to brand our identity with a constant reminder that He must get bigger and we must get smaller. And we purposefully (if slightly confusingly) lettered our name as one word using lowercase type. Again, we were just reminding ourselves that sixsteps is not about any one artist but rather a family (all one word), and that it's not about us (lowercase) but about His glory.

> ## He must get bigger and we must get smaller.

The way we figure it, the world doesn't need more stars—because the Story we are a part of already has one. But with being an artist, musician, or band come photo shoots, album covers, stages, media interviews, and possibly awards. So, how do we keep from acting like stars when we are standing in the light? Simple. Stay in love with Jesus, the main character in our story. If He really is our

Star, the challenge is not so much to shun the spotlight (if you're really good at what you do, you can't dodge recognition, anyway) as it is to redirect any light that comes our way onto Him. If we make this our aim, success is redefined. We know we're moving in the right direction when people see that our eyes are on Him, and in the end that leaves them clamoring for His touch more than ours.

And I'm not talking about the cheesy and over-the-top finger-pointing-to-heaven kind of aiming people toward Jesus. Rather, a genuine reflection of Him that becomes more real the closer you get to someone, that transferable sense of authenticity that is cultivated and refined in the presence of the Almighty. Sure, none of us are fully there, and the flesh is always willing to make a stand, but how refreshing to see the most talented businessperson, scholar, artist, educator, athlete, mom, and so on carrying themselves with an unforced and genuine preference for Jesus and His glory.

The more we happily point to Jesus, the more we know that Sabbath rest has taken root in our hearts. That's why Sabbath rest (and the weekly embracing of a day to consider again just how great God is) is true and uncorrupted worship at its best. For when we tirelessly toil, as though that's what it takes to keep our ship afloat, we steal God's glory, elevating ourselves as sole providers and sustainers of all we have and are. By refusing to slow down and bring things to a halt, we are telling God that He is not enough for us. Sure, we may sing the songs of praise and mouth words about His vast and sovereign control, but our failure to remember the

Sabbath is nothing more than foolish pride, arrogance gone wild, and mistrust unfurled—the very opposite of what worship is all about.

That's why worship and Sabbath go together. By ceasing from our efforts when God asks us to, we make much of Him. When we trust Him by resting in Him, we exalt Him, championing Jesus as all-powerful by our purposeful inactivity.

Furious rest, you see, is not about doing nothing. It's about doing everything we do with the quiet confidence that our lives, families, business, ministries, relationships, and record labels are in His hands.

Maybe for you the circumstances are different, yet the weight is the same. You know, the weight of trying to make yourself out to be bigger than you are—the stress of trying to figure out how to run your life on your own, of always trying to determine the outcome, control the relationship, close the deal, run the show, hold it all together, know the future, protect your interests, build your kingdom—the weight of playing the role of God in your life and the lives of those around you.

But be encouraged. Today is the Sabbath. Oh, it may not literally be Sunday (or whatever day you hold sacred in your tradition), but Sabbath is a state of mind and attitude of the heart. Sabbath happens anywhere and everywhere we let go of the controls and lay the cares of our lives at His feet.

So, where is your future right now? Where is the outcome of

your pressing dilemma? Is it in your hands? Is it in the hands of the businessman or woman on the other side of the table? Is it in the hands of a boyfriend or girlfriend? In the hands of a team of doctors?

Or is your life, and all that concerns you, in the hands of Jesus, the One who constructed the universe effortlessly in one week?

If you want more *rest* and less *stress,* declare this very moment to be your Sabbath—the place where you pry your fingers off the circumstances and people you are trying so desperately to control, the place where you discover that life really does work better in His hands than it does in yours.

Embracing Smallness

God put Sabbath in every week for a reason. And the looking up we do on that first day of the week must bear fruit in all the moments of every other day for us to stay connected to the reality of *I am not but I know I AM.*

It's a small thing, but for several years the screen saver on my cell phone read *"iamnot,"* a subtle but constant reminder of the freedom I have found in being small, a reminder I need much more than I'd like to admit.

For me, embracing smallness is not a one-time proposition but a daily event. That's why in Eden there wasn't one big Sabbath to end all Sabbaths. God knew how strong the undertow of sinful pride would be. He knew how quickly we would read and believe our own press. That's why a seventh day of rest has anchored each week from the beginning of time, and why Sabbath is still calling us to the end of ourselves today.

I have found that I can easily say (and teach) "I am not but I know I AM" all day long, but words are cheap and life is hard. Sure, the fruit of this "little me, huge God" truth is amazing. Who wouldn't want a life marked by "glorious death" and "furious rest"? But to mean it when I say that I want my life to count for His glory is to drive a stake through the heart of self—a painful and determined dying to me that must be a part of every day I live. That's what Paul was getting at when he said, "I die every day."[1] He was declaring his intention to come to the end of himself before he came to the end of his life—to die to self-power and self-glory long before they put his body in the grave.

> ## Pride is simply an admission that I haven't seen God at all.

If there's one thing we can all be sure of in our quest to live for His glory and His fame, it's that the flesh will not die quietly. No, our mortal selves will scrape and claw for every ounce of self-promotion they can get their hands on. Whenever an opportunity presents itself, the voice of pride will rise up with a roar, urging us to take control. Whenever a spotlight is near, our flesh will run toward it and attempt to soak it in. That's why, like Paul, we must carry around an attitude of death everywhere we go, a moment-by-moment willingness to abandon the self-life—to let it die—no matter what the cost.

Humility—another word for knowing my name is *I am not*—can be described as "seeing God as He is." Pride is simply an admission that I haven't seen God at all. Humility is the instant rightsizing of me that occurs with just one eyeful of His Majesty. True humility (not the false kind that ends up being about us at the end of the day) is not a sign of weakness, failure, or inability, but rather a sign that we are getting to know God and have glimpsed His glory. And once we see how glorious His glory really is, we realize that all other glory is futile and fading and totally inconsequential in the grand scheme of things.

One thing that's helped me look up this past year has been a book titled *The Universe: 365 Days.*[2] Based on the same premise as the picture-of-the-day website that NASA hosts, the book is comprised of a calendar and a cosmic photograph for each corresponding day. I have used it as a part of my daily approach to God for almost a year. Every now and then there's a picture of an astronaut or spacecraft, but I skip over the celebration of what humankind has made and go right to the good stuff—the truly mind-stretching stuff of heaven that literally stops me in my tracks. On more than one occasion, I've had to close the book and put it down because my brain simply couldn't compute the immensity and complexity of what I was seeing.

Say you didn't want to take the full 365-day journey; you could just check out September 23. The accompanying photo and text show our sun, a raging ball of fire, as it rocks our solar system with heat and light, converting its mass into energy at a staggering rate equivalent to 100 billion nuclear bombs exploding every second.

Or flip back to January 14, where you'll find the Ring Nebula. This gaseous ring (a collection of dust and gas) is positioned in such a way as to allow us to look straight down its barrel and through to the other side. The hot gases toward the inside are a cobalt blue, cooling to fantastic hues of green, yellow, and red as they expand to the ring's farthest edges. The photo shows a tiny white dot in the open center. This dying star is emitting the gas that forms the massive and mesmerizing tie-dyed ring of the Ring Nebula (and inspired for me the phrase "glorious death").

Or check out October 4. There you'll find my personal favorite, NGC 628, the perfect spiral galaxy, a picture-perfect marvel containing hundreds of billions of stars floating through space about thirty million light-years away from earth.

You get the idea, right? Simply looking up into God's heavens seems to shrink whatever my day holds to a more manageable size...and reminds me once again of His great size.

But it's not just the expanse of the cosmos that helps me remember my smallness and God's bigness every day. Really old things make me feel small. Like the pyramids. Or the Sistine

Chapel. Or when I consider that hundreds of generations have passed before me and not a single person among them ever knew my name.

Mysterious things make me feel small too. Mysteries like the conception of human life and the sovereignty of God. Like eternity.

> We are tiny bundles
> of nanometer-sized
> components, yet people
> infinitely loved by God.

And often the tiniest of things make me feel smaller still, things like the subparticles of subparticles that make up the intricate building blocks of the matter that forms earth. Like the stuff of nanotechnology, an area of science dealing with real-world applications of activities at the level of atoms and molecules. Nanotechnologists are dealing with small, *really small*. As it turns out, a nanometer is one billionth of a meter (a meter is about the length of your arm), or about one eighty-thousandth the diameter of a human hair. Somehow, knowing that people are measuring things in nanometers, and actually constructing useful things that are tens of thousands of times thinner than one of my hairs, makes me feel…infinitesimal.

That's what you are and I am—infinitesimal. Tiny bundles of nanometer-sized components, yet people infinitely loved by God.

When you get right down to it, trading in the little story of me is not really all that big of a sacrifice, after all. Who wouldn't want to abandon a script you could fit on the pointy end of a pin for a chance to get in on the glorious epic that is so enduring that its screening will require all of eternity? Glimpsing His glory makes me want to say, "Your name and renown are the desire of [my soul]."[3] Seeing His true fame makes me want to live for a bigger purpose, doing everything I do in such a way as to shine the spotlight on Him.

But how do I do that daily? How do I live for His name in the daily grind?

Well, the answer is not easy, but it is simple—you do whatever it is you do in such a way as to reflect His character to the world around you. You don't have to be a preacher like John or Paul, or a missionary, or a worship leader, or a Christian record label–type, or a church worker. In fact, you may even have a better shot at amplifying His glory if you're *not* any of those things. Everyone expects pastors and ministry types to live for a bigger story, but how cool is it when people in every walk of life do what they do with a greater purpose in mind?

That's why Paul wrote, "*Whatever you do,* whether in word or deed, do it all in the name of the Lord Jesus, giving thanks to God the Father through him."[4]

Paul is saying that living for God's glory is not so much about *what* you do as it is about doing *whatever* you do in such a way that it reflects Jesus Christ to those around you and ultimately points people to Him. In other words, you don't have a better chance of glorifying God by being a preacher than you do by being a bond trader, or by being a missionary versus being a mother. You don't get more credit in the kingdom of God for being a songwriter than you do for being a student.

And what does that kind of Christ-exalting life look like? For starters, being the best at what we do, leading in every strata of society, being honorable and dependable, walking with humility, and treating everyone we encounter along the way the same way Jesus would.

And how would we know when we have slipped back into the story of us? We know when we see these telling signs:

- When I live like I'm privileged, I have lost the plot. In other words, when I start acting like I deserve a certain outcome or a higher standard of life, I have failed to strike the fatal blow to self and am living like I actually have rights in this world apart from God.

- When I am demanding, I have lost the plot, insisting that God and others meet my needs on the timetable that I see fit.

- When I act pompous, I have lost the plot, thinking that I am somebody while only proving that I haven't had a good look at God today.

- When I crumble under the pressure, I have lost the plot, declaring that the outcome of life rests squarely on my shoulders, not His.

- When I start protecting, I have lost the plot, marking turf as though it were actually mine and forgetting that everything I have comes first from above.

- When I crave the spotlight for myself, I have lost the plot, losing sight of the Story line and the One True Star. And every time I do it, I waste one of life's fleeting chances to make my life truly count by amplifying Him.

- When I fail to celebrate the successes of others who are living for His fame, I have lost the plot, thinking that possibly we are on different teams when we actually share supporting roles in the same story.

- When I dwell on feelings of being unloved, unnoticed, or insignificant, I have lost the plot, abandoning the miracle of knowing God on a first-name basis.

To die to self is to gain on an unfathomable scale.

All these privileged, demanding, arrogant, frazzled, turf-protecting, glory-stealing, self-loathing moments are nothing more than a clarion call alerting us to the fact that it's time to die again, reminders that the life of smallness requires a vigilant watch and a constant willingness to strike the fatal blow in the heart of me. But to die to self is to gain on an unfathomable scale—a daily funeral that is nothing more than the doorway to a life filled with the matchless wonder of all that God is.

Jesus Christ—the great *I AM* come to earth—understood this well, being willing to shed His heavenly glory for a spot in God's redemptive Story. He was willing to fully give of Himself so that ultimate glory could come to His Father.

Because He knew there was a greater glory to come, Jesus was never petty, pompous, demanding, or defeated—no matter what circumstance He faced. Just the opposite. He kept giving Himself away so others (including you and me) could taste true greatness in a relationship with God.

"Less of Me and More of God."

Thus, Jesus defines a Christ follower (Christian) as one who models His lifestyle, one who will "deny himself and take up his cross daily and follow" Him.[5] He, too, knew that embracing smallness and crucifying the flesh is something we must do every single day.

That's why the ultimate expression of smallness is the death of self. It's the ultimate end that comes after the prayer "Less of Me and More of God."

To be honest, looking up doesn't make life's challenges and problems go away. Yet gazing into heaven reassures me that God still is *I AM* and that His greatness, goodness, and Godness is the best lens through which to view every day of my life.

You Can Trust Him

Follow the signs to the intensive care unit in the hospital of your choosing and the scene will be very much the same as at any other ICU anywhere else in the world. Camping out in waiting-room chairs, families will be hunkered down day and night, a new-found community of strangers, all with one common bond—clinging to hope for those they love. Through the doors and down a restricted corridor are mothers and fathers, sons and daughters, husbands and wives, relatives and friends—all clinging to life.

It was already past dark when a friend dropped me off at Piedmont Hospital in Atlanta after a flight from Texas. Since I'd grown up nearby, it was a place I knew all too well. On a muggy summer night when I was eleven, my dad and I had come through the emergency room doors, my fibula broken clean in two. It's also the place where my grandmother died. Walking through the main entrance, I wasn't sure what to expect. A few days before, on Valentine's Day, my mom had reached Shelley and me while we were in Colorado with her family. The news was somewhat murky and a lot unsettling. My father, who she thought had been ill with the flu, had suffered a seizure and was in a coma-like state.

Our choice was to either have the surgery or face death.

Nothing was conclusive at last report, but things were serious enough that I knew I needed to get to Atlanta as soon as possible. My dad was in ICU, which obviously meant he was in critical condition. But just how critical I would soon discover. I hadn't been at the hospital for long when my mom and I were huddled in a tiny consultation room adjacent to the ICU waiting area with a neurosurgeon. A release form was on the little table, awaiting our signatures. My father had contracted viral encephalitis, a one in one hundred thousand occurrence when a blood-borne infection breaks the code on the body's lock on the nervous system and, ultimately, attacks the brain. My dad had a life-threatening infection…in his brain. By now, it was almost too late to save him.

As the doctor delivered this news, I felt numb. I was hearing his words, but I was wondering if I was awake or asleep. I was scrambling to catch up to the reality of what he was saying. He went on to say that my dad's brain was swelling at an alarming rate, his fever was spiking, and it wasn't likely he would live through the night without a radical procedure.

The doctor was asking for our consent to an operation that would remove a significant portion of the infected area of my dad's brain, decompressing the area and allowing more room if the swelling persisted. Our choice, he said confidently and without emotion, was for my dad to either have the surgery or face certain death.

Is this really happening? I thought. *These are our choices?*

I was thirty years old and staring at a form that would potentially decide my father's life.

It was two in the morning when my dad came out of the operating room, and I had purposefully staked out a place in the hallway where I guessed they would roll his bed between the OR and the ICU. His eyes were open, and mine were fighting back tears as I told him how great he did in the surgery. Amazingly, he recognized me and said, "Hey, Ace." I knew something superinvasive had happened to my dad, and his head was heavily bandaged, as you might expect, but he knew who I was. That was something to take comfort in through the night.

They were moving him fast, but I managed to grab on to his hand and tell him we were camped out in the waiting area and would be there all night long.

God saved my dad's life that night, but the suffering was just beginning.

To fast-forward a bit, God saved my dad's life that night, but the suffering was just beginning. One night in the ICU waiting room turned into three weeks as the little clumps of chairs and tables became our home away from home. My dad didn't leave Piedmont until two months later, and only then to transfer to an inpatient rehab hospital across town. He was cured of the infection but devastated by its effects. Sometime after the surgery, he suffered a stroke, and the resulting left-side paralysis, compounded by the permanent effects of the brain swelling that impaired his vision and cognitive skills, left my dad disabled for life. He would never drive again, dress himself, return to work, swing a golf club, or do the one thing he was truly genius at—create art. As it turned out, unbeknownst to us, the part of my dad's brain they had to remove that night was the part where artistic ability resides.

While my family's story and yours are not identical, I expect you can relate. Like me, you have walked through places so deep and dark that your faith is rattled at the core—the place where we secretly, and not so secretly, wonder, *If God is so great, and the loving I AM, why doesn't He intervene, stop the suffering, end the pain, restore what's lost, halt the march of death?*

If you haven't yet come to such a place, you will. Sooner or later we all find ourselves at the midnight crossroad—a crisis of trust, when the sky turns black and life seems to spin out of control. That's where our friend John the Baptist ended up not long after his encounter with Jesus at the Jordan River.

John's outspoken criticism of King Herod's marriage to his brother's wife did not sit well with the king or his new wife. So the king had John arrested and thrown in prison. While John wasted away wondering when or if he'd ever be released, he heard glowing stories of the miracles Jesus was performing and of the large crowds that followed Him everywhere.

Time passed.

John waited.

Finally, John asked two of his followers to take a question to Jesus: "Are you the one who was to come, or should we expect someone else?"[1]

What John really wanted to know was, *If You are who I think You are, then why am I stuck in this jail? Why don't You come and perform one of Your miracles for me?*

We've all been there, wondering if God really is who we think He is. And if He is, why doesn't He come and change our circumstances?

And what happened for John? Jesus sent a reply: "The blind

receive sight, the lame walk, those who have leprosy are cured, the deaf hear, the dead are raised, and the good news is preached to the poor."[2] All signs pointed to the fact that Jesus *was* in fact who John thought He was. But for reasons beyond our understanding, Jesus did not perform a miracle for John. He didn't even visit his prison cell.

And then for John, the worst happened. During Herod's birthday party, the order was given for John to be beheaded—a senseless murder at the whim of the king's stepdaughter.[3]

You'd think that if God were going to come through for anybody, He'd come through for John the Baptist. But He didn't. In fact, from where we're sitting, it looks like Jesus let him down completely, standing by, doing nothing, while evil, cruel people took John's life.

If we're honest, many of us have felt the same way.

How can we trust God when darkness falls?

And, just as the scriptural account doesn't neatly resolve John's plight, so our circumstances often don't resolve in this life either. Every situation doesn't have a tidy conclusion, and sometimes we are left with nothing but faith. But what do we put our faith in when it *looks like* Jesus is not coming through for us? How can we trust God when darkness falls? Where do we turn when our prayers seemingly go unanswered? And above all, how do we reconcile our belief in a good and gracious God with the seeming void of anything good or gracious in our present circumstance?

Well, I know what we can't do. We can't just stuff the questions inside for fear our asking will make us appear to doubt God or make us look unspiritual. And we can't just dole out generic answers like "We need to just trust God" and "You know, God's ways are higher than ours." It's 100 percent true that our lives are to be lived by faith…and equally true that we could never fully grasp the plans of God. But there is something more to hold on to in the most painful storms of life, namely the Cross of Jesus Christ.

The Cross is not simply legend or story. It occurred at a real place, at a real moment in time, where the Son of the living God—*I AM* in human form—suffered and died. From a human vantage point, the day Jesus died was easily the worst day on earth. Everything that could have gone wrong went wrong. The innocent was accused. Justice was skewed. A mob went wild. Soldiers drove nails through His hands and feet. His agony was great, as for hours He struggled to breathe. In the end, the sky turned black and, feeling alone and abandoned, Jesus died.

In that moment the scene at the Cross screamed,

- "It's not fair!"
- "This is a mess!"
- "Somebody do something!"
- "This is the worst possible outcome!"
- "Everything's gone mad!"
- "Jesus is a fraud!"

- "God is dead!"
- "The darkness has won!"

Yet God was not absent that day. He was very much at work, accomplishing something bigger than any of us could have conceived if we were standing in the moment. For what appeared to be a senseless murder was actually divine intervention. And, when it seemed that God wasn't powerful enough (or good enough) to stop the chaos, God was actually being both big enough and good enough to orchestrate our redemption through the sacrificial death of His only Son. Never before had the world seen love like this—God reaching down to do the dirty work of buying back our lost souls in the most staggering act of grace and mercy ever seen.

Though it seemed like violent men ruled the day, the purposes of God were being fulfilled. And while it's true His Son was abused and killed, the Father was using the pain to do the most beautiful thing that has ever been done. An innocent man went to the cross, but a guilty one died there, Christ becoming sin for us, so that we could become the righteousness of God in Him.[4] The hands of men may have strung Jesus up to die, but only the work of God could offer Him up as a sacrifice for our sin. As Peter proclaimed in his message to a Jerusalem crowd soon after the death and resurrection of Jesus, men were involved but God was in charge all along.

> Listen to this: Jesus of Nazareth was a man accredited by
> God to you by miracles, wonders and signs, which God

did among you through him, as you yourselves know. This man was handed over to you by God's set purpose and foreknowledge; and you, with the help of wicked men, put him to death by nailing him to the cross. But God raised him from the dead, freeing him from the agony of death, because it was impossible for death to keep its hold on him.[5]

God never lost control at the Cross, and He's never lost control of you either. In fact, from our vantage point, the Cross echoes an entirely different message, shouting,

- "God is at work!"
- "Grace has come!"
- "Love has won!"

The Cross of Christ is the place where trust in God is born, lighting the way through the valley of the shadow of death. What looked like the worst day in history is now the source of our praise. The death and resurrection of Jesus Christ is an act of kindness from a loving and trustworthy God, an undeniable demonstration of His goodness that we can cling to when our sight and understanding fail to make sense of the circumstances that surround us. The Cross is the place where we anchor our hope when all seems lost. And the Cross is the source of our praise when we cannot see through darkness.

My dad beat the odds and survived encephalitis. And for this mercy we are forever grateful. But though he lived, the landscape for our family was dramatically and irreversibly changed. What followed were years of intense challenge and heartache. And while we prayed and contended for supernatural intervention and miraculous healing, more often than not it seemed the very opposite outcome became our reality.

Dad's original stay at Piedmont was followed by multiple others—once with a broken back from a car crash, then a broken hip and replacement surgery from a fall, others because of feeding-tube issues, and, on the night I want to tell you about, a recurrence of the infection that had originally attacked his brain. During this stretch, he was in constant pain and there was absolutely nothing any of us could do about it. It was late on a Sunday night, and I was due for a flight back to our home in Texas. I gently kissed my dad on the forehead and walked down the corridor toward the elevators. Once I was inside, the doors closed and it was as if hope were closing as well.

Once more I was fighting back tears. I was alone and frustrated and helpless. "God, I have asked You before, and I'm asking again: please do something miraculous and heal my father tonight," I cried. "I don't know if You will, but I know You can." I had taken this elevator ride and prayed this same prayer too many times to count, but on this night something happened. A spirit of defiant trust filled my heart.

All of a sudden, in my mind's eye, the Cross came into view. While God had not moved in many of the ways we had hoped for regarding my dad, He had done something: He had marked history and eternity with His love and grace. And He watched His

Son suffer brutally and die…for us. I knew in that moment that my heavenly Father, like no other, fully understood my pain and my family's pain. And I believed that He loved us.

My heart was heavy, but I chose to praise God right then and there. My eyes were filled with tears, but somehow through the tears, I blurted out loud, "God, I choose to worship You in the dark." And with every ounce of me I said, "Let it be on record that I trust You no matter what and I will praise You no matter what the outcome."

Soon the plane carrying me home was airborne over Atlanta and making an unusual departure out of the city. I was shocked as we banked low and hard over downtown and directly over Piedmont Hospital. I can't say, in all my years of flying, that I have been on a flight taking this particular path. I was glued to the window as we passed overhead, our ascent making the lights of the hospital smaller and smaller. I could almost make out the fourth-floor windows that included my dad's room, and in my mind I could see through the walls and imagine him as I had left him an hour or so earlier. And then the whole building shrunk beneath us and eventually out of sight.

The Cross was proof, and I was clinging to it.

For me, it was if God was assuring me. Sure, the immediate confines of my dad's room were filled with chaos and pain, but my loving Father was above it all, seeing far more than my family could see or understand. He was both in the dark night with us and already in the dawn of what would eventually come. He was in the moment holding us, but also over it all, loving us. The Cross was proof, and I was clinging to it.

I'd love to tell you that my defiant praise changed the circumstances that night, but I honestly don't know all that God was doing in those hours. And I'd love to tell you that I always get it right when hardship comes, but I don't. Yet what I am reminding us of is this: God never loses control. When all else fails, the truth of Christ's Cross may be all we have, but it is enough to fuel our confident trust in *I AM*.

Like with John, we don't always know how the pieces fit together. But in the shadow of the Cross, we do know that *they do fit together.* And we know that while Jesus chose not to intervene in John's arrest, He knew full well the details of His own. Had John been released from Herod's grasp, he would have been shocked to see this very Jesus hanging on a tree. And he would have come face to face with the overcoming truth that God uses everything for our good and His glory.

As we've discussed, the skies declare that *I AM* is huge, but the Cross of Christ affirms that *I AM* has the best interests of every *I am not* in mind. Our God is in the heavens, and the whole world is under His command, but now because of Christ's death and resurrection, we can personally know how much He loves us, believing that on the worst day of all, He was displaying the most beautiful gift of love the world will ever see.

After seven years of struggle, a heart attack took my dad away from us. I wish I could fully explain how his suffering and God's glory merge. But that will have to wait until we see Jesus face to face. But I can say this: God brought us through. And He worked in and through it all in ways that still baffle me. In the season of Dad's death, much of what Shelley and I are giving our lives for today was born. I could write another book about our relocation to Atlanta (all spurred because of my father's illness), the subsequent confusion when, just before our arrival, he died, and the ensuing chapter of life where vision was born out of the crucible of adversity. From the fire came a confident calling, the ballast of a movement that has literally taken us around the world.

None of this makes what we went through any easier, nor does it cause our journey to make more sense. But it does remind us that Someone higher is always writing a greater Story—a Story that will endure when all else fades. We are living in the shadow of the Cross and in the power of an empty tomb, believing in light of these that "our light and momentary troubles are achieving for us an eternal glory that far outweighs them all." For as the apostle Paul wrote, "We fix our eyes not on what is seen, but on what is unseen. For what is seen is temporary, but what is unseen is eternal."[6]

This is why I am urging you to exchange the starring role in your small story for a supporting role in our God's epic adventure. It's time for you and me to live as those who can never be the same because we have encountered both the great power and the great love of *I AM*.

And in the days to come, when you're questioning, needing, searching, wondering, asking, and struggling, you will find His sufficiency at the end of every desperate prayer. When you cry out all the things that you are not, you'll know His answer is "I AM."

For every cry, there is one answer:

"I need help."

I AM.

"I need hope."

I AM.

"Who could possibly be smart enough to figure this out?"

I AM.

"What works?"

I AM.

"What lasts?"

I AM.

"What's the latest thing?"

I AM.

"What's the hippest thing?"

I AM.

"I need a fresh start."

I AM.

"I need a bigger story."

I AM.

"My vision is bigger than my resources."

I AM.

"Nothing's real anymore."

I AM.

"Who can I trust?"

I AM.

"I'm not sure who's on my team."

I AM.

"Nobody's listening to me."

I AM.

"I don't have a prayer."

I AM.

"My marriage is sinking, and I don't know where to turn."

I AM.

"I can't hold on."

I AM.

"My kids deserve more."

I AM.

"I'm pouring into others; who's pouring into me?"

I AM.

"If we fail, who will get the job done?"

I AM.

"I'm not sure why I'm here."

I AM.

"I've given all I can give and it's not enough."

I AM.

"I'm tired."

I AM.

"I quit!"

I AM.

"I can't!"

I AM.

"I need a drink."

I AM.

"I need a fix."

I AM.

"I need a lover."

I AM.

"Somebody just hold me."

I AM.

And what does this great *I AM* say of Himself? He says to you and to me, "I am the Way, I am the Truth, and I am the Life. I am the Resurrection and the Life. I am Savior. I am Jesus—the Solution, the Restorer, the Builder, the Answer, the Wise One, the Coming One, the Mighty One. I am the Lord and there is no other. I am God and there is none besides Me. I am the First and the Last. I am Alpha and Omega. I am the Beginning and the End. I am the Lord, that is My name, and I will not give My glory to another or any of My praise to idols. I AM WHO I AM, and that is My name—My memorial name to every single generation."

The One-Word Bible Study Method

The One-Word Bible Study Method (OBSM) isn't an official name, just one I have created for myself. Given that much of the chapters "Became" and "The Journey" are built around the OBSM, it might be a good idea to talk through what the method is about and how it works.

A long time ago, through a seminary friend, I encountered the discipline of observation, or looking intently at a given object over an unusually long period of time. The approach is based on the famous teaching method of Louis Agassiz, a scientist who taught at Harvard during the nineteenth century. He regularly asked his students to look carefully at a fish (a preserved lab specimen), then write down a description of what they saw. When students thought they had noticed everything, they'd report their findings to the professor. But he would say, "No, no! You haven't seen it yet! Start over!" and send them back to study the fish again. This process of observing, writing down findings, reporting—and starting over again—would often last every day, all day, for more than a week.

Here's the thing: with each commitment to further observation, Agassiz's students made fresh discoveries—layer upon layer of greater detail, and deeper and more important insights than they would have ever noticed the first few times through.

We have to immerse ourselves in His Word.

Applied to the study of Scripture, the discipline of observation means that we look intently into the text for an extended period of time, waiting for the text to begin to breathe and disclose its meaning. Too often we speed-read through the text, underline a key phrase here or there, and move on without giving the living Word enough time to take root in our hearts and reveal more of what it's about. But Paul wrote, "Let the word of Christ dwell in you richly as you teach and admonish one another with all wisdom, and as you sing psalms, hymns and spiritual songs with gratitude in your hearts to God."[1] If we are going to know God well, and walk in intimate fellowship with Him, we have to immerse ourselves in His Word. It is the living expression of who He is to you and me.

In a sense, the OBSM is nothing more than meditation—allowing God's Word to slowly soak into our minds and hearts. The OBSM is *not* a substitute for conventional Bible study methods (exegesis). I'm not even saying that the OBSM should be your primary Scripture study path. But after you've applied a more traditional study approach (for example, an inductive Bible study, where you ask of the passage, "What does it say? What does it mean? And how do those two things connect with my life?"), I think you'll find the OBSM extremely helpful for getting even more out of the text.

The OBSM works better with some types of literature than others. The history books, the prophets, and the narratives found primarily in the four gospels don't usually work as well as the epistles (the bulk of New Testament teaching books), where the content is presented in logical sequence.

I have done large chunks of Scripture in the OBSM style. For example, the book of Romans. The OBSM caused me to stop and park for a while on the very first word, where otherwise I would have probably kept on reading. Romans 1:1 opens with the word "Paul." For me, that name became a one-word summary of the entire book of Romans. Why? In a sense, all of Romans is depicted by the life story of this man, a hater of Christians and a persecutor of the church who was changed by God's sovereign grace from Saul into Paul, the writer of much of the New Testament and the first century's most effective mouthpiece for the gospel.

Every word in your study may not be spectacular, but many will be, making the whole process worthwhile. As you find a verse or phrase you want to focus on and absorb, write it down on something you can carry with you. Read the passage one word at a time. Focus on each word until it starts talking back to you. After a while, you will probably see things you have missed many times before. Patience is the key. You can't rush the process, and you can't make the words tell you what you want to hear. Listen to them and let your knowledge of all Scripture speak into what you're discovering in this particular passage.

I would have never observed *BE* in *beloved* or in *became* if I hadn't spent a lot of time wrapping my mind around the idea that God's *I AM* name also translates as *BE*.

BE Can Be a Beautiful Thing

My use of *BE* as a personal devotional idea has helped open up other larger scriptural themes for me as I've studied verses in context. But, right off the bat, it's important to acknowledge its limitations.

For example, I understand that the use of the letters *be* in front of another word (as in the case of *became*) to imply *I AM* is a personal interpretation, not a meaning inherent in the word itself. After all, *be* as a prefix has at least a dozen different meanings in its various verb formations in English, and many *be* combinations have no devotional implications at all. (I'm also aware that my personal interpretations get lost entirely when *be* words are translated into other languages.)

But if you're an English speaker and are up for it, consider that a few years ago I was speaking at a conference for teens. After one of the main sessions, a high school student came up to talk with me. She was a pretty typical sixteen-year-old—jeans, flip-flops, a couple of layers of tees and tanks, and a small corduroy shoulder bag slung low below her waist with a wide strap that she tugged on with her left hand. A couple of small button pins dotted the shoulder strap, one of which she was now detaching and holding in her hand as a four-foot-wide smile crossed her face, welling tears suspended in her eyes.

About the size of a quarter, the bright red pin boasted in bold uppercase letters, "I AM LOVED." Anticipating her words, I reached out and took hold of the pin. "I just wanted you to have this," she said. "It's what you talked about tonight during the message. Thank you for reminding me how much God loves me and cares about me. I'm going through some really hard stuff in my life right now, and I really needed to hear that again tonight."

Beautiful!

In that session we had been digging into the first three verses of 1 John 3. Even though most of the kids at the camp were using the New International Version of the Bible (a very readable translation, phrased with language that reflects the idioms of modern culture), I had been teaching from the New American Standard Bible. I am somewhat attached to the NASB because I used it in the formative years of college, seminary, and beyond, and because the word sequence and word choices are truer to the original text in many instances than the NIV. On this night teaching from 1 John, I wanted the NASB word choice because it made this passage come alive in a much better light.

The chapter begins with this stunning proposition: "See how great a love the Father has bestowed on us, that we would be called children of God; and such we are." And it continues, "Beloved, now we are children of God."[1]

You and I are BE loved.

Granted, "Beloved" sounds a little churchy, and it's not a word we use in our culture except at weddings and funerals. That's why the NIV has substituted the words "Dear friends." But "Dear friends" doesn't work so well for me if the alternative is "Beloved." I'll take "beloved" any day!

And you should too.

Beloved, as you know by now, is a compound word made up of the two words *be* and *loved. BE,* as we have already discovered, equals *I AM.* Thus, *beloved* translates to *I AM* loved. And that's who we are. You and I are *BE* loved.

That night we talked about how the word *beloved* could be used as a statement of fact, as in "You are beloved (I AM loved) right now whether you feel it or think you deserve it. Right now, because of what God has done through Christ, you are beloved."

But we also talked about how *beloved* is a command, as in

"Be loved!" In this sense, God is the first mover, and He is not really asking us to allow Him to love us as much as He is telling us to receive what He has already demonstrated in the death of His Son.

Well, this girl got it that night. Imagine her surprise when she looked down and saw that "I AM LOVED" pin staring back at her, an affirmation of the message God was writing on her heart.

In a way, the whole story of the gospel and the Christian life can be told by a handful of *BE* words.

Beloved.

Became.

Beheld.

Behold.

Because.

Be still.

Even the Beatitudes are now the *BE* attitudes (the God attitudes or *I AM* attitudes), as *I AM* once again appears in His Word.

Start

1. Exodus 3:14.
2. See Matthew 16:26.

Divine Invitation

1. While Moses was certainly unqualified in many respects, it is also true that he was the product of the Egyptian royal establishment (perhaps the only Hebrew with such an upbringing) and, as such, providentially equipped to understand the requirements of leadership that this task would entail.
2. Exodus 3:4.
3. Exodus 3:5.
4. Exodus 3:7–9.
5. See the formidable list of *-ites* in Exodus 3:8.
6. Exodus 3:10.
7. Exodus 3:11.
8. See Exodus 3:11.
9. Exodus 3:12.
10. See Exodus 3:13.
11. Exodus 3:14.
12. Exodus 3:15.

Light Flies

1. In fact, the universe is so big that scientists need measurements even greater than the light-year. For these distances, they use a parsec, which equals 3.26 light-years, or a little more than 19 trillion miles.
2. Psalm 33:6, 9.
3. Isaiah 40:22, 25–26.
4. 2 Peter 3:8.

Became

1. Luke 4:18–19.
2. Luke 4:21.
3. John 8:58.
4. See Colossians 2:9.

The Journey

1. See Romans 6:23.
2. Ephesians 2:4–7, ESV.

God's Passion for God's Glory

1. Micah 6:8.
2. Genesis 1:1.
3. Psalm 90:2.
4. Isaiah 40:22; Psalm 19:1, NASB.
5. Psalm 148:3–5.
6. Philippians 2:11. Sadly, most people think this magnificent proclamation about the suffering Servant and His ultimate

rule and reign ends with the exclamation "every knee should bow...and every tongue confess that Jesus Christ is Lord" (verses 10–11). But the passage actually proceeds from there to the conclusion, "to the glory of God the Father," underscoring that the end of the life, death, resurrection, and eternal rule of Christ is the exaltation of God and His glory.

7. Isaiah 42:8.

8. Romans 1:21–23, 25.

9. James 1:17.

10. Notice Exodus 14:17–18: "I will harden the hearts of the Egyptians so that they will go in [the sea] after them. And I will gain glory through Pharaoh and all his army, through his chariots and his horsemen. The Egyptians will know that I am the LORD when I gain glory through Pharaoh, his chariots and his horsemen."

Big River

1. Genesis 11:3–4.

2. Philippians 2:5–11.

The Little Leader

1. John 1:19.

2. John 1:20.

3. John 1:21–22.

4. John 1:23–27, italics mine.

5. John 1:29, NASB. In this verse, the New International Version translation fails us, and I reach back for the trusted

New American Standard Bible of my youth. The NIV
inserts the word "Look," a fine verb and an appropriate
thing to say when your desired end is to cause people to see
something. But the NASB's "Behold" (and, yes, I understand that we are talking about semantics, not exegesis)
puts John's confession in a whole new light.

6. John 1:30.

7. John 1:36, NASB.

8. See John 1:37.

9. John 3:26.

10. John 3:27–28, italics mine.

11. John 3:29–30.

12. John 3:31.

Be Still

1. Mount Sinai is also known as Mount Horeb, the place
   where Moses had his initial encounter with God at the
   burning bush.

2. See Exodus 33:18–23; 34:29–35.

3. Exodus 20:8–11, ESV.

4. Psalm 46:1, 7, 10.

5. Genesis 1:1–2.

6. Genesis 1:3–5.

7. Colossians 1:27.

Furious Rest

1. See Acts 9:1–31.

2. Colossians 1:27, 29, NASB.

3. The name was inspired by King David's attempts to return the Ark of the Covenant to Jerusalem. Read about it in 2 Samuel 6:12–15.

Embracing Smallness

1. 1 Corinthians 15:31.

2. Robert J. Nemiroff and Jerry T. Bonnell, *The Universe: 365 Days* (New York: Harry N. Abrams, 2003).

3. Isaiah 26:8.

4. Colossians 3:17, italics mine.

5. Luke 9:23.

You Can Trust Him

1. Luke 7:20.

2. Luke 7:22.

3. See Matthew 14:1–12.

4. See 2 Corinthians 5:21.

5. Acts 2:22–24.

6. 2 Corinthians 4:17–18.

Appendix A

1. Colossians 3:16.

Appendix B

1. 1 John 3:1–2, NASB.

GRATITUDE

I'd like to thank Don Jacobson, who got me into writing in the first place; my editor, David Kopp; and all at WaterBrook Multnomah for helping carry this message farther than I ever could alone.

The concept of making much of the glory of God was first shaped in me when I heard John Piper speak in 1994. My view of life was forever altered from then on. Thank you for unpacking the equation of our satisfaction and God's glory in our generation.

So many spurred me on—assisting, offering insight, and sustaining this project with their prayers: my assistant at the time, Jennifer Hill; Carrie Allen and all at Passion/sixstepsrecords; Benji Peck; Gabe Lyons; Stuart Hall; Matt Redman; Thomas Womack; Jennie Graves; and Terry Willits. Your words of belief keep me believing too.

As the reprint became a reality, my navigator, Brad Jones, stepped in and managed the essential details that make it possible for a project like this to become a reality. As well, Leighton Ching, helped shape the direction for a new cover, and Gary Dorsey came through with a simple yet bold design.

Shelley, my bride and partner, I love you! You're the best thing that ever happened to me, and everything I do is better (not to mention possible) because of you. You are my joy in the journey.

All praise to Father, Son and Spirit Divine.

Louie Giglio / *I am not*